This series offers the concerned reader basic guidelines and *practical* applications of religion for today's world. Although decidedly Christian in focus and emphasis, the series embraces all denominations and modes of Bible-based belief relevant to our lives today. All volumes in the Steeple series are originals, freshly written to provide a fresh perspective on current—and yet timeless—human dilemmas. This is a series for our times. Among the books:

How to Read the Bible
James Fischer

How to Live Your Faith
L. Perry Wilbur

A Spiritual Handbook for Women
Dandi Daley Knorr

Temptation: How Christians Can Deal with It
Frances Carroll

With God on Your Side: A Guide to Finding Self-Worth Through Total Faith
Doug Manning

A Daily Key for Today's Christians: 365 Key Texts of the New Testament
William E. Bowles

Walking in the Garden: Inner Peace from the Flowers of God
Paula Connor

How to Bring Up Children in the Catholic Faith
Carol and David Powell

Sex in the Bible: An Introduction to What the Scriptures Teach Us About Sexuality
Michael R. Cosby

How to Talk with God Every Day of the Year: A Book of Devotions for Twelve Positive Months
Frances Hunter

God's Conditions for Prosperity: How to Earn the Rewards of Christian Living
Charles Hunter

Pilgrimages: A Guide to the Holy Places of Europe for Today's Traveler
Paul Lambourne Higgins

Journey into the Light: Lessons of Pain and Joy to Renew Your Energy and Strengthen Your Faith
Dorris Blough Murdock

EIGHT STAGES OF CHRISTIAN GROWTH

Human Development in Psycho-Spiritual Terms

PHILIP A. CAPTAIN

Prentice-Hall, Inc., Englewood Cliffs, New Jersey 07632

Library of Congress Cataloging in Publication Data

Captain, Philip A.
   Eight stages of Christian growth.

   (Steeple books)
   "A Spectrum Book."
   Includes index.
   1. Christianity—Psychology. I. Title. II. Series.
BR110.C337 1984   248'.01'9   84-8236
ISBN 0-13-246679-1
ISBN 0-13-246661-9 (pbk.)

All biblical verses are taken from the
King James version unless otherwise noted.

This book is available at a special discount when ordered
in bulk quantities. Contact Prentice-Hall, Inc., General
Publishing Division, Special Sales, Englewood Cliffs, N.J. 07632.

1 2 3 4 5 6 7 8 9 10

Editorial/production supervision by Chris McMorrow
Cover design by Hal Siegel
Manufacturing buyer: Frank Grieco

ISBN 0-13-246679-1

ISBN 0-13-246661-9 {PBK.}

Prentice-Hall International, Inc., *London*
Prentice-Hall of Australia Pty. Limited, *Sydney*
Prentice-Hall Canada Inc., *Toronto*
Prentice-Hall of India Private Limited, *New Delhi*
Prentice-Hall of Japan, Inc., *Tokyo*
Prentice-Hall of Southeast Asia Pte. Ltd., *Singapore*
Whitehall Books Limited, *Wellington, New Zealand*
Editora Prentice-Hall do Brasil Ltda., *Rio de Janeiro*

Contents

Foreword

A saying that has made its way into popular culture is "You are what you eat." The author of that phrase was promoting good eating habits, reasoning that what we take into our bodies by mouth affects how we look, act, and feel.

But, actually, we are not what we eat. We are what we think. There is a Proverb that says, "as he thinketh in his heart, so is he . . ." (Proverbs 23:7).

Our world view, our philosophy, our belief in God, or our disbelief in God colors everything that we are and everything that we do. There is no person without a world view based on his or her concept of ultimate truth or reality. Flowing from the individual's world view or concept of truth is a multiplicity of values, political beliefs, and philosophies. It is ludicrous to suggest, as some do, that those who do not believe in God are more pluralistic, more tolerant, and more open-minded than those who do believe in God. The non-Christian has his set of beliefs that flow from his concept of ultimate truth, just as the Christian does.

Like the body, which responds negatively to the ingestion of bad food or the breathing in of polluted air, the mind, also, reacts according to that which it consumes. "Garbage in, garbage out" may be a simplistic way to put it, but essentially that is the way the mind works.

The Apostle Paul set the ideal: "Be not conformed to this world, but be ye transformed *by the renewing of your mind*" (Romans 12:2). This means that an unrenewed mind is something to be avoided. Our conclusion must be that the actions that flow from an unrenewed mind are not the ideal which God has designed for that mind.

There is no conflict between intellect and faith. But there is and always will be conflict when man attempts to replace God with his own reasoning and to substitute his own ideas for God's eternal truth. This is what modern psychology has done, and this is why it is floundering.

In rejecting outright the "secular medicine chest," with its myriad potions that never seem to cure the disease but only treat the symptoms, Dr. Captain calls for nothing less than a return to man's ultimate source of truth—the Bible as the Word of God.

His contention is that man has been looking in the wrong place for the solution to his psychological problems and, therefore, has constructed a secular psychological system to address essentially spiritual needs.

This is a book that will shake the foundations of the psychological establishment, as it offers a radically new Christian alternative to the theories of secular psychology. Every Christian who is committed to working with and helping people achieve spiritual wholeness needs to read this book.

Jerry Falwell

Preface

As an academic discipline, psychology came into existence because Christians failed to define and understand adequately the human existential condition. It is only because people in the church were unable to find the answers to the existential questions of life that they turned to the modern-day priests of secular humanism—secular psychologists, psychiatrists, and social workers. These professionals have been trying to rebuild society and save man through human logic, effort, and reasoning, and today we can see clearly that they have failed. In spite of all the money, time, and effort that governments and academic scholars have put into the field of psychology and its offshoot, the mental health system, there is more psychological sickness today than ever before. Today, the mental health system is fighting a losing battle to save people and our society. In the midst of the chaos, it is time for Christians to rise up and offer a solution that is real—the solution of a changed life through Jesus Christ.

This book rejects the idea of accommodation with secular psychology. Christians are not to accommodate themselves to the world. Today too many Christians are seeking answers to spiritual questions from secular men who have constructed secular theories. While it is acknowledged under the concept of common grace that there is probably some truth in these theories, there is also an extensive amount of error. Because most people find themselves unable to distinguish between the truth and error, they have become a subtle means through which people have been deceived and led away from God's Word.

This book also rejects the idea of integration that is presently circulating among Christians. Over the last few years many books and papers have been written by Christians in an attempt to integrate secular psychological theories with Biblical principles. Somehow, it was out of this merger that we tried to build Christian psychology. The problem is that integration, while good, has not proven to be enough. There is still a separation between the Christian theologian and the Christian academic psychologist. There is still a separation between the Christian counselor and the Christian minister. Although integration has led many Christians to become involved in the mental health system, it has not been able to create a radically new approach to counseling or to stop the process of psychological decay that we see presently in our society. As Christians, we need to go beyond integration.

This book attempts to construct a Christian theory out of Biblical concepts and Biblical data. It is hoped that this theory will help us reach out to a psychologically and spiritually lost world and help people to become truly whole again.

What I am presenting is not just one man's ideas, but God's truths. I realize that this is a somewhat grandiose claim, but all I can ask is that the reader examine the ideas with an open mind and test them against the Word of God.

My goal is to discover the truth about man as revealed to us by God. Therefore, I welcome discussion and debate and am willing to change any idea that can be shown to be contradictory to Biblical teachings. My life is dedicated to glorifying God and being His servant, and I hope that through this effort we can understand Him more as we come to understand ourselves better.

1

Christian Stages of Development

Within the field of psychology there are several theories that specifically attempt to deal with human development. Two of the best known
are Sigmund Freud's theory of the psychosexual stages of development
and Erik Erikson's theory of the psychosocial stages of development.
Freud attempted to discuss human development as it relates to human
sexuality, which implies that it is man's sexual needs that are most important to our understanding of psychological health. Erikson, who believed that Freud placed too great an emphasis on human sexuality, felt
that man is primarily a social being and that the need for relationships
goes beyond just the need for sex. Freud, then, focused more upon man
in the biological dimension, while Erikson focused upon man in the
social dimension. While Erikson contributed significantly to our understanding of human development, especially in the area of expanding
his stages of human development to the entire life span, there is still a
basic missing ingredient in his theory.

We acknowledge, as did Freud, that man is a biological being,
but as Christians we believe that we are more than just a body. We also
acknowledge, along with Erikson, that man is a social being in need of
human relationships, but this is still an insufficient viewpoint for

1

building a theory of human development that will help us understand man's most basic psychological needs. The missing element in both of these theories is the fact that man is at root a spiritual being created by God in His image. The basic needs of man are primarily spiritual in nature. To discover what these spiritual needs are, we must understand the nature of Our Creator, His will and His purpose for man's existence, and the created potential placed within man by God. The primary source of our information on these subjects is the Bible. The goal is to discover a series of psychospiritual stages of development that can then be used to replace the secular theories as the basis for our understanding of the human developmental process.

The first approach that could be used by Christians to find and develop such a theory would be to look for a specific passage of Scripture that clearly delineates Christian stages of growth and development. However, all of the passages in the Bible that refer to such a developmental process have inadequacies. First, these passages refer to the process of Christian growth and maturity without tying it to the human chronological life span. For example, a Christian is exhorted to move from a babe in Christ, drinking milk, to an adult who eats meat (Hebrews 5:12–14). In reality this process of becoming more spiritually mature is not necessarily related to one's chronological age. Second, passages referring to divisions of life do not provide a specific enough base upon which we could build psychospiritual stages of development. For example, in I John 2:12–14, the life span is divided into the categories of children, young men, and fathers. As a result of the inadequacies of specific Scriptural passages, most scholars conclude that a theory of psychospiritual stages of development does not exist.

This book, however, is based on the premise that a psychospiritual theory does exist, that it can be found within the boundaries of the Bible, and that it can be used as a blueprint for our understanding of the human developmental process. The core idea for our Christian theory of development is built upon the concept that the Bible is a progressive revelation of God that corresponds with the process of human development over a person's entire life span. Each Biblical era has not only a specific historical meaning, but also an additional meaning in relation to the psychological growth of human beings. The primary premise upon which this book is built is the idea that God, through the gradual unfolding of the historical account of His dealings with man from the beginning of time to the end, was also informing us about the gradual unfolding of each single human life, from conception to physical death. If this premise is true, by examining the different stages or dispensational eras found in the Bible concerning God's dealings with man we can obtain a guide to our understanding of the psychological development of children and adults.

The next section of this chapter will be concerned with establishing the different Biblical eras and specifying the developmental stages that correspond to each. A chart is located at the end of this section to identify more clearly the relationship between the Biblical eras and the human developmental stages.

BIBLICAL ERAS

Garden of Eden

The first era we find in the Bible is associated with Adam and Eve in the Garden of Eden. In the Garden man and woman were without sin and in perfect fellowship with God. Adam and Eve were in a state of oneness with God as they walked and communed together. Adam and Eve were also totally dependent upon God for the environment in which they lived and the meeting of their needs. In this way life in the Garden of Eden corresponds with the first stage of a child's life, which is as a baby in the womb of its mother. In our theory this stage of human development is called the *Innocence Stage*.

The womb symbolizes the perfect environment in which the fetus is in perfect fellowship or oneness with the mother. In the same way, Adam and Eve were one with God in the Garden of Eden. The baby in a mother's womb is in a state of total dependency for the oxygen, blood, and food that give it life. Because of this total dependency, the baby is in a state of total innocence in relation to sin and to its future.

It is not being suggested here that the account of Adam and Eve is just a myth and that only the act of human birth is real. It must be reaffirmed at this point that, although a secondary meaning is being given to Biblical events as we connect the Biblical eras to our developmental stages, we are not in any way attacking such events as no longer being historical. I believe in the inerrancy of Scripture, which means that Adam and Eve were real, the Garden of Eden was real, and the fall of man through sin was real.

The final connection between the baby in the womb and Adam and Eve in the Garden is the fall of man. In the same way that Adam and Eve experienced the trauma of being separated from God when they sinned, a baby experiences the trauma of separation from its mother when it is born. Being born then is associated with the shock that was experienced by Adam and Eve when they had to leave the Garden. Both had to leave a sheltered world and enter a world that required struggle to survive and forced them to deal with the problem of pain and suffering.

Adam to Noah

The second Biblical era found in the Bible extends from Adam outside the Garden to the time of Noah. This corresponds to the first developmental stage of life outside the womb of the mother, the *Nurturance Stage,* which runs from birth to approximately the age of two.

The term *nurturance* is used in relation to this stage because the infant at birth is completely unable to directly meet his or her own needs. After the umbilical cord has been severed, the basic needs of the child are no longer met. What is now required is a nurturing figure who is willing to meet the baby's needs. In other words, in order to survive the baby needs the physical and psychological nurturance of a mother or mother substitute. Second, from a psychological perspective, during this stage the child is completely egocentric. This means that the child sees him- or herself as the center of the universe, with the world revolving around him or her. At this time the child is unable to delay gratification without experiencing frustration, and there is no concept of right and wrong and no conscience. Because of this, the child must be loved and nurtured unconditionally out of benevolence because the child is unable to meet the mother's needs or expectations directly.

In relating this developmental stage to the Biblical era from Adam to Noah, we can see that God's dealings with man were also on the basis of benevolence and unconditional nurturance. Genesis 6:5 indicates to us that at this time "every imagination of the thoughts of man's heart was only evil continually." Mankind, like the newborn baby, was in a state of complete egocentrism after the fall. In the dispensational era from Adam to Noah, God had to nurture mankind unconditionally because man was only evil continually. At this point, there was no conscience and no law. As a result, God decided that through Noah and his seed He would go on to the next stage, and the means He used to destroy evil, degenerate mankind was the flood.

Noah to Moses

The third Biblical era goes from Noah after the flood to the giving of the law through Moses. This era corresponds to the third stage of a child's development, which runs from age two to six and is called the *Obedience Stage*. In developmental terms the flood symbolizes the washing away or destroying of the memories of the first two years of a child's life. By this we are suggesting that, for the good of the child, God destroys all of the memories of the Nurturance Stage and blocks them from coming again to conscious awareness. In saying this we are in disagreement with psychoanalytic counselors who suggest that they can take people's memories back to the birth trauma, into the womb, or back to a previous life. These are all counterfeit experiences. A child cannot remember these first years because of a lack of a language system.

After the flood God promised that He would never again intervene in the world in that way "though the imagination of man's heart is evil from his youth" (Genesis 8:21). Instead, in Genesis 9:11–14, we find God establishing a covenant with man and providing a symbol of this covenant in the form of the rainbow. In developmental terms, God establishes a covenant with all children as they enter the Obedience Stage in that He establishes the "law written in man's heart" (Romans 2:15) or conscience. The conscience given to the child at around age two is a symbol of God's covenant with that child. Through this conscience each child can now begin to distinguish between right and wrong, and language is the tool that makes this possible.

This means that the Obedience Stage begins as the child begins to use language as a form of communication. The most important developmental task during this stage is that the child through the conscience learns to choose to be obedient to his or her parents. While the mother is the most prominent figure in nurturing the child, the father takes the lead disciplining and training the child. The child begins this stage with a strong assertion of negative will at age two and ends it, hopefully, by learning how to control it by age six. The focal point in this process of learning to obey is the concept of trust or faith. The goal is willing obedience of the child due to a trust in the father's authority.

In the Biblical era from Noah to Moses the best example of these principles of trust and obedience can be found in the person of Abraham. The Bible tells us us in Hebrews 11:17 that "by faith Abraham, when he was tried, offered up Isaac." Abraham's faith led him to willingly obey the Father because he trusted Him. In the same way it is important for children to learn to trust and obey their parents. Ephesians 6:1 tells us, "Children, obey your parents in the Lord, for this is right." Therefore, willing obedience to parental authority is the goal of the Obedience Stage.

Moses to the Prophets

The fourth Biblical era extends from the giving of the law to Moses on Mount Sinai to the rise of the Prophets. It was in this period, commonly referred to as the *law stage,* that God established human law, human government, social order, and social responsibility. Notice that, according to the Bible, the concept of government and laws was not a human creation but originated with God. God created law and government, and God gives government its authority and people their rights. Without God, law deteriorates to anarchy and government is destroyed.

The primary principle that we must teach our children in the fourth stage, the *Behavior Stage,* is that there can be no social order without law and that law has its final authority in God. The primary focus of the Behavior Stage, extending from the age of six to age twelve, is that the child must learn responsibility. A job must not just be done, it should be done well and without complaining. It is during this time that the child should begin to shoulder part of the weight of being a member of a family by learning how to contribute as well as take. This is also a time of life when the child needs to begin to learn the difference between right and wrong behavior and to develop skills and talents. Therefore, the Behavior Stage centers upon what the child is doing. It is different from the Obedience Stage in that the focus there was upon not doing wrong. Here the focus is upon how to do right as the child is taught the laws of society and the laws of God.

As we associate the Behavior Stage with the Biblical era from Moses to the Prophets, we find that God here is primarily concerned with teaching His people to follow the law covenant, which was centered around making them more socially responsible to each other as well as to Him. This concern is reflected in the Ten Commandments in such statements as "Thou shalt not kill"; "Thou shalt not steal"; and "Thou shalt not bear false witness" (Exodus 20:7–17). Just as God was trying to teach the children of Israel social responsibility through His law, parents must also teach their children, as they go off to school, how to live in harmony with others. Positive goals during the Behavior Stage are those of teaching children how to cooperate, share, and give.

Prophets to Christ

The fifth Biblical era centers around the message of repentance. This message was the same for all of the Prophets, up to and including John the Baptist. Jesus summarized this message when He said, "Repent ye: for the kingdom of heaven is at hand." (Matthew 3:2). The emphasis during this period has been changed by God from one of pleasing Him by following the law to guilt before the law. As the Bible clearly teaches us, no one was able from his or her heart to follow the law completely and thereby please God—"All have sinned and come short of the glory of God" (Romans 3:23). As a result, following the law was no longer enough. God now demanded that man acknowledge his imperfection, sin, and guilt and that he repent.

This Biblical era corresponds with the *Motive Stage* of human development, which extends from age twelve to age twenty. The emphasis during this period is no longer upon the law as an arbitrary, externally imposed set of rules, but upon the concept of the law as a personally meaningful standard imposed upon the self. This is a transition stage between law and grace, where the concept of personal guilt before the law is of central concern. Having taught the child the laws of God and society in the Behavior Stage, the parent must now stand back and gradually let the child begin to make more and more judgments and choices on his or her own. In this way the adolescent can begin to develop personal responsibility for what he or she chooses to do and become accountable for the decisions. Although many of these choices might be considered unwise or foolish by adults, to deprive the child of the right to make his or her own mistakes is to hinder the child's growth.

During the Motive Stage the child develops an internal value system by which he or she can become a responsible adult. There are two primary problem areas, however, that confuse the child during this stage. To go forward, the adolescent must first come to understand his or her inner self. One aspect of this process of self-discovery involves understanding one's emotions. Adolescents in the Motive Stage must learn to identify and eventually control the internal emotional states that arise from their relationships with other people. The second major problem concerns the issue of motives. The adolescent must also learn that within the heart of man there is a problem with motives. In the Behavior Stage the child only had to be concerned about what he or she did. Now in the Motive Stage he or she must also learn that more important than what we do is why we do it. Eventually all must learn that our motives are primarily evil, which leads to sin and, thereby, produces a state of guilt and condemnation as we stand before God. This problem of guilt can be dealt with only through a belief in the sacrificial atonement of Christ's shed blood on the cross.

God the Son

The sixth Biblical era centers around the person and work of Jesus Christ, including His sinless life, His innocent death, and His victorious resurrection. The purpose of His life was the salvation of mankind. Man had been given the law; he internalized its meaning, but still found himself unable to live up to its standards. Jesus Christ came to establish a higher order than judgment under the law, which is the concept of God's grace and forgiveness. In this stage, however, man must go beyond repentance to a changed life through a commitment to the cause of Christ. Grace allows us to be set free from the bondage of the law and the bondage of guilt by allowing us to change our perception of ourselves from a negative one to a positive one through the Lordship of Christ in our lives. The focus for the disciples was shifted from a burden for self and the needs of self to a burden for the world and the needs of others. Through this commitment a person's life can take on a new, much deeper purpose and meaning. "And ye shall know the truth, and the truth shall make you free" (John 8:32).

The sixth stage of human development is the *Meaning Stage,* which extends from twenty to thirty years of age. The primary concern of the young adult who is moving from childhood to adulthood is one of "Who am I and where am I going?" The central question that must be asked by every young adult concerns what is to be the meaning and purpose of his or her life. Initially this question seems to be centered around the role that we are choosing to play in life. The focus is on such issues as what to major in at college, which job would be most satisfying, and who would make the best marital spouse. Eventually we must come to see that it is not the role that we work within that gives our life meaning, but the cause to which we are committed. As Chrsitians, our highest commitment should be to Jesus Christ as our Lord and Savior. Therefore, the Christian view is that true fulfillment in the Meaning Stage can only be found by committing ourselves to the cause of Christ.

God the Holy Spirit

The seventh Biblical Era began when Christ sent the Holy Spirit into the lives of the disciples at Pentecost and continues today through the work of the Holy Spirit ministering to the needs of the world. This era is referred to as the *church age*. The primary purpose behind the sending of the Holy Spirit was to give the followers of Christ the power of God with which to turn the world upside down. This power is centered in God's agape love, as shown in I John 4:12,13, where it is stated that "If we love one another, God dwells in us and His love is perfected in us. Hereby know we that we dwell in Him and He in us, because He hath given us of His Spirit."

The confirmation of our commitment to the Lordship of Christ is that Christ sends His Holy Spirit to dwell in us. We become the church as we share the power of God's love with the world around us. Therefore, it is the Holy Spirit that teaches us how to love ourselves, to love our neighbor, and to love God. Without the Holy Spirit, there is no power in our Christianity and no love in our hearts, with the result being that the Gospel message is not given to the world.

In terms of our developmental stages of life, this era corresponds with the *Love Stage*. In using the word *love,* we are going beyond the usual human interpretations of the word as sexual desire or an emotional state. We are referring to agape love, which is the power of God to heal people's lives and make them whole. This stage runs throughout most of our adult life, but occurs primarily between the ages of twenty-five and forty-five. The goal during this period of life is to be able to establish meaningul adult-to-adult relationships with people. This can be done through friendships, a job, a marriage, church involvement, and other activities that bring us in contact with others. To love and be loved is a universal need created in us by God. The impact of our life is measured by the effects that our life has upon those whom we are closest to in terms of interpersonal relationships. Therefore, in the Love Stage not only do we need to learn how to be close to people, we also need to work on making sure that in this closeness people's lives are more enriched.

God the Father

The eighth and final Biblical era centers around the concept of our eternal state after the end of time. The Bible indicates that the will of God is detemined by God the Father. The Father brought the world into existence. The Father cast Adam and Eve out of the Garden because of man's sin. The Father sent His Son Jesus Christ into the world for the redemption of mankind. Finally, the Father will judge the world and all that is within it. All of us will someday be judged by God the Father as to what we have done with our lives. Through this judgment each person will pass from temporality into eternity and the judgment made by God the Father will determine our eternal fate. The Bible teaches that there is spiritual life after death. The two possibilities for man are either eternal life and existence with God, or eternal death and separation from God. The Bible also teaches that this physical world as we know it will be destroyed and that God the Father will create a new heaven and a new earth and those whose lives have produced fruit for God will be allowed to dwell there (Matthew 7:17–20).

The last developmental stage, the *Fruit Stage,* extends from approximately forty years of age to the end of one's physical life. There are two concerns that arise within this stage. The first concern is in relation to an individual's particular role or identity. For the person approaching their fifties, the issue begins to become one of what he or she has accomplished in life. The person looks back over his or her life and wonders whether there was any value to his or her existence or whether it was all just vanity. The hope is that through the many years of effort something has been contributed that will be of value to the world. The second concern relates to the personal relationships that one has had. The focus is upon the impact that one's life has had upon others, especially family members. Through an examination of the way an individ-

Biblical Era	Biblical Stage of Human Development	Age Range
Garden of Eden	Innocence	Baby in Womb
Adam to Noah	Nurturance	0–2
Noah to Moses	Obedience	2–6
Moses to Prophets	Behavior	6–12
Prophets to Christ	Motive	12–20
God the Son	Meaning	20–30
God the Holy Spirit	Love	25–45
God the Father	Fruit	40–

ual life has been lived, one hopes to find something to make all the struggle and pain worthwhile. In this way a person tries to generate his or her life out into the future and thus to defeat death. From a Christian perspective we cannot defeat death, since that was done by Christ on the cross. We know that it is only through serving God and sharing His love with the world that we can solve the problem of death by transcending it as we move into eternal life.

HIERARCHY OF BASIC HUMAN NEEDS

Seven basic human psychological needs can be associated with the stages of human development. In the field of psychology, Abraham Maslow introduced the "hierarchy of basic human needs," which progresses from a concern for one's physical needs to the need for self-actualization. This hierarchy has two major deficiencies. The first is that the terms at the top of his list, the need for self-esteem and the need for self-actualization, are never adequately defined. Christians especially must reject self-actualization as Maslow defines it because man's need for salvation is never taken into account. In other words, Maslow's list is constructed on a humanistic philosophy of life where man supposedly has the innate capacity and goodness to fulfill his potential, yet even by Maslow's acknowledgment few people ever reach what he calls self-actualization.

The second problem with Maslow's hierarchy of basic human needs is that it is totally disassociated from the developmental process. Even if we could define what it meant to be self-actualized, there is no indication within his theory of how to get there. The hierarchy is not related to the developmental stages of life, so we don't know when to focus on what need and how to go about fulfilling it.

The hierarchy of basic human needs being developed in this book takes into account both of these problems. First, each need will be clearly defined so that everyone will be able to understand what it is and to identify whether it is being met presently in their life. Our list of needs also takes into account the Biblical teaching that man lives in a state of conflict between good and evil rather than only being basically good. As a result, when we discuss the hierarchy of basic human needs again in later chapters, we will find that there is tension at every step in the hierarchy between the positive and negative ways that human beings try to fulfill these needs.

Second, our hierarchy of basic human needs will be directly related to our developmental stages, making it possible to know what need should be focused upon the most at any given point in a person's life by first identifying that person's stage of development. This also gives us the ability to identify whether that person is at the appropriate stage of development or fixated somewhere in the developmental process. If we can do this, it allows for a major theoretical breakthrough in terms of Christian counseling. Up until this time, Christian counseling has focused largely on technique. But, with our Christian developmental stages and the Christian hierarchy of basic human needs, we will now be able to focus on the process of Christian counseling using an adequate theoretical base.

The seven basic human psychological needs that have been developed to correspond with our Christian stages of human development will only be presented in brief form in this chapter, so that the readers can see their importance more fully as they read through each of the individual stages in the next section of the book.

DEVELOPMENT AND THE
BASIC HUMAN NEEDS

Nurturance Stage

A child's first stage outside of the womb is the Nurturance Stage, which runs from birth to approximately the age of two. The focus is upon a mother figure meeting her baby's basic physical and psychological requirements in order for growth and development to take place. The nurturing of the infant is done unconditionally since the baby has no capacity to give back directly. This leads us to the basic human need for the Nurturance Stage, which is *Security*. The need for security is defined here as the state the infant experiences when his or her needs are adequately met. Security is based on the feeling of being special. This specialness is not to be determined by what the child does but by what the child is—a miraculous creation of life involving the parents and God. All children should be considered special at this point, regardless of their abilities, sex, characteristics, or handicaps. Security, therefore, is based on the concept that all children are special because life is special. Life is special because it is a miracle of God. Security also relates to a confidence that we can have that because we are special someone is concerned about making sure that our needs will be met.

Obedience Stage

The second stage of life outside the womb is the Obedience Stage, which runs from the age of two to the age of six. During this stage the father takes responsibility for teaching the child the principle of obedience to his authority. Within the child's drive for autonomy and self-exploration, the child has no concept of danger. As a result, without the protection of limits established by a loving authority figure, the child will eventually hurt him- or herself.

This leads us to the second basic human psychological need—the need for *Liberty*. Children need freedom. They need the freedom to grow, to be themselves, to learn. A question being debated within our society today concerns how best this freedom is to be obtained. Secular humanistic philosophy teaches that freedom and authority are incompatible concepts. The argument presented is that if you have authority there is no freedom, and that freedom can only be obtained through the destruction of authority. This book presents a different viewpoint. By tying liberty to the Obedience Stage, we are proposing that true freedom and loving authority must go together. It is the child whose father establishes safe limits and guidelines for him or her to live within who ends up being the most free.

Behavior Stage

The third stage of development outside the womb is the Behavior Stage, which runs from approximately six to twelve years of age. It is within this stage that the child shifts from not doing wrong to learning how to go about doing things right. The emphasis during this period is on learning and skill development. This leads us to the primary need of the Behavior Stage, which is *Competency*. The need for competency is based on the idea that all children need to feel they are a success. Because our society evaluates people on the basis of being the best, to be a success a child must compete with other children and in this competition always must come out on top. The Christian view disagrees with this approach. Success through competency stems not from being the best but from doing your best. Instead of teaching children to compete with each other, we need to teach them that their primary competition is with themselves. In this system, effort becomes more important than performance, and all children can become winners. All parents thereby become responsible during the Behavior Stage for helping each of their children find some special area in which he or she can develop competency and feel like a success.

Motive Stage

The fourth stage of life outside the womb is the Motive Stage, which covers all of the adolescent years from approximately age twelve to age twenty. In this stage, focus must shift from the child's behavior to the child's inner self—the mind and the heart. The Motive Stage is a time of confusion as the adolescent begins to try to understand his or her own thoughts, feelings, and motives. Because of the uncertainty of this process of self-discovery, the teenager begins to think of him- or herself as unusual or abnormal. This leads the adolescent to seek some kind of affirmation that he or she is okay, first from parents and then from peers. We can now see that the primary need of the Motive Stage is *Acceptance*. The need for acceptance is initally tied into what other people think of the person. All teenagers want to feel that they are normal and that people like them. Problems arise when adolescents do not feel accepted by the people around them. A lack of acceptance by others leads to a willingness by teenagers to change their values and beliefs if they feel someone will like and accept them. This approach to meeting the need for acceptance is destructive. Adolescents must learn that true acceptance begins only when we can learn to accept ourselves. We do this by being ourselves as God created us, not by trying to be something that we are not.

Meaning Stage

The fifth stage of life outside the womb is the Meaning Stage of young adulthood, covering roughly age twenty to age thirty. In the Meaning Stage each person is struggling to define his or her adult identity and role in life. The young adult is seeking to find out what his or her destiny in life is to be. This is a time to plan, to dream, to hope. One's whole future lies ahead and the potential seems unlimited. The primary need in the Meaning Stage is for *Commitment*. Each young adult must find a cause in which to believe. It is through this cause that life takes on a purpose. Without commitment, the young adult will begin to drift. Initially, the cause begins as an idealistic possibility. Hopefully, by thirty the cause will have been translated into a workable form that is more realistic. The greatest danger of this stage is disillusionment, caused by an inability to translate one's idealistic dream into a workable form. When this happens, commitment is lost and life becomes dull. In the end the amount of meaning that we feel our lives have is directly related to the type of cause we find ourselves committed to by age thirty.

Love Stage

The sixth stage of development outside the womb is the Love Stage. To some extent this stage overlaps with the Meaning Stage which precedes it, and the Fruit Stage which follows it. For most, the Love Stage centers around marriage and the family unit, although adult friendships can also be quite important to many people. The emphasis changes from one's role in life to one's relationships with people. The need for relationships is part of the nature of man as created by God. We all need to relate. Therefore, the primary need of the Love Stage is *Intimacy*.

Intimacy is associated with being physically, psychologically, and spiritually close to people. Today too many of our attempts to fulfill our need for intimacy take place only on the physical plane of human sexuality. An assessment of society shows that many people are seeking love, but very few are actually finding it. Marriage relationships are less satisfying, the divorce rate is climbing, and homes seem to be falling apart. The Christian perspective is that the need for intimacy must be fulfilled on the spiritual plane first in our relationship to God. As we experience God's love for us and develop an intimate relationship with Him, we can begin to experience more true intimacy in our relationships with others.

Fruit Stage

The seventh stage of life outside the womb is the Fruit Stage. This stage begins at a point in life when people begin to spend more time looking backward and reminiscing than looking forward and planning. In the Meaning Stage, the question focused upon is "What will I do in life?"; in the Fruit Stage, the question asked is "What have I done?" This is a time for reflection and evaluation. In this process many people find themselves feeling depressed because they did not fulfill their original dream. Therefore, the primary need associated with the Fruit Stage is *Value*.

Every person has the desire within themselves to live a life that is significant. No one wants to think that what one did was meaningless or futile. We all want to be important. We all want to be remembered. Very few people, however, achieve or accomplish great things. As Christians we know that the value of one's life is not determined by what is written about us in the books of men, but what is written about us in the book of life, which will be read when we stand before God.

The following table lists our hierarchy of basic human needs and shows their relationship to life's developmental stages.

Biblical Stage of Human Development	Hierarchy of Basic Human Needs	Age Range
Nurturance	Security (To Be Special)	0–2
Obedience	Liberty (To Be Free)	2–6
Behavior	Competence (To Be Successful)	6–12
Motive	Acceptance (To Be Liked)	12–20
Meaning	Commitment (To Have A Cause)	20–30
Love	Intimacy (To Be Close)	25–45
Fruit	Value (To Be Remembered)	40–

2

The Process of Development

The purpose of this chapter is to establish some basic principles that can be used to aid us in understanding the developmental process. Although nothing in this chapter will be specifically related to any of the stages in our Christian theory of human development, these basic principles will actually apply to all of the stages. The questions we will concern ourselves with here are: How does the process of development unfold? How do we go from one stage to the next? What effect does one stage have on the others? Why do we have stages of development in the first place; is not every person unique?

The issue that we must deal with is the nature/nurture controversy within the field of psychology. How much of what we are and what we do is controlled by givens that exist from the beginning, and how much is controlled by the process of living and experience? The word *nature* in this discussion implies that we are born with something. The word *nurture* implies that it is learned. This chapter will focus on discussing two issues related to this debate. The first section will deal with the concept of developmental stages and the implications of these stages for raising children and working with people in counseling. The second section will deal with the concepts of maturation and learning and how these relate to our understanding of life's growth process.

DEVELOPMENTAL ASSUMPTIONS

In this section we will be making three basic assumptions in relation to the developmental process. These assumptions can then be used to help us more fully understand our Christian theory of development. We can also use these assumptions to discuss how to identify problems in the growth process so that help can be obtained.

Distinct Stages

The first assumption with human development is that *there are distinct stages of development universal to all children and adults.* There are two key terms in this assumption. The first is the word *distinct,* which implies that you can distinguish a person by his or her psychological struggles and conflicts within the chronological age sequence of life. To say that there are distinct stages forces us to define what these stages are and clearly show that the stages are different from each other.

The second key word in this assumption is the word *universal,* which implies that every human being not only goes through distinct stages of development but that they go through the same series of stages. The concept of the universality of the developmental stages supports the Christian view that man was created by God. If one were to believe in evolution, within this evolutionary process it easily would be possible for different human beings in different parts of the world to have come up with different psychological stages of development. In this hypothetical situation the stages of these different races would be distinct within the racial subgroup but would not necessarily be universal to all racial groups. The very fact that the developmental sequence of human growth is universal is evidence to support the theory of creation. This means that as we discuss our Christian theory of human development we can assume universality, because God created all people of every race the same.

Therefore, our first assumption is that all people go through the same distinct stages. It happens this way because it was God, not man, who established these stages. As Christians understand these stages, we can more adequately use them to raise our children and to develop higher levels of spiritual maturity. We can also see that if it was God who established the developmental stages it would be highly improbable for God to step in and intervene in the developmental process. Our conclusion must be that God wants us to use the development process rather than ignore it or try to escape it. This principle is especially important for the spiritual instruction and training of our children. What we must learn in relation to human development is not only the right thing that must be done but also the right time to do it.

Specific Order

Our second assumption is that the stages of development *come in a specific order and build on each other*. In other words, human development is not a random process. Not only are there distinct stages of development that every person of every race goes through, they go through them in the same sequence. The fact that the stages come in a specific order allows us to be able to predict and/or anticipate the developmental tasks and needs at any given point in a person's life. By being able to predict this process, we are then more able to meet those needs fully and to diagnose when a person in the process of development has run into problems. Finally, this same predictablility will help us to aid people more effectively when they need psychological counseling.

It might be pointed out that not all individuals enter or leave stages of development at exactly the same time. By itself, the fact that there are variations in chronological age when different people complete a stage does not destroy the predictability of the stage or the predictability of the sequence. We obtain flexibility within our system of predictability by use of the bell-shaped curve. It has been found that there is a normal statistical distribution in which we use the mean to define the general parameters of our developmental stages. As a result, the specific order and time of our developmental stages are determined by the approximate chronological age at which most people enter or leave a stage. This allows for the possibility that, age-wise, a person could be either ahead or behind the norm and still be within the normal sequence. At some point, however, there is a bottom limit below which no child could go or the whole concept of a developmental sequence would be destroyed. Technically what we have then is not a perfect bell-shaped curve but a skewed distribution with a distinct cut off or limit on the bottom.

If we can assume that the human developmental stages come in a specific order and that development is not a random process, the only element that is needed in order to build a theory of development is some basis for a particular sequence of stages. In this book that basis is the concept that the Bible unfolds in a series of stages or eras. These dispensational eras of the Bible unfold in a series of distinct steps that come in a specific order, which corresponds with the human developmental process. This means that our blueprint for understanding human development now has its basis in God's truth and not man's thinking.

Optimum Time

The third assumption that needs to be made about human development is that there is *an optimum time for dealing with the psychological task associated with each stage.* If each stage is distinct, according to our first assumption, there is a specific psychological need that must be dealt with at each developmental stage. In the first chapter the primary psychological task associated with each stage was presented in terms of our hierarchy of basic human needs. In the same way that the developmental stages unfold in a specific order, the basic human psychological needs unfold in a specific order, and the best time to deal with a particular psychological need is during the stage it is in primary ascendency.

This leads to several secondary assumptions that accompany this idea of an optimum time.

First, within the limits of the developmental stages, *no psychological task can be completed before its optimum time.* There is a readiness involved in the developmental process. Until the child or adult is maturationally ready to complete a particular psychological task, he or she will be unable to do so. One of the reasons why this is true is because the stages of development build on each other. As a result, the person is not ready to focus on the psychological need of the next stage until he or she has had a sufficient amount of time to fulfill the need of the previous stage. For example, children cannot learn to run until they have first learned to walk, since walking necessarily precedes running.

Second, *any psychological task not completed during the optimum time for that task will be more difficult to complete later.* For example, we know that there is an optimum time at which children can learn to walk, ranging from approximately nine to fifteen months of age. If, for some reason, the child is not able to learn to walk during this period, perhaps because of sickness, the task of learning to walk becomes much more difficult. In terms of reading, the same is true. There is an optimum time ranging from approximately five to seven years of age when children can most easily learn to read. We know, however, that if a child does not learn to read during this period of time, the skills of reading will be much harder to learn later. In terms of our hierarchy of basic human needs, this means that each need has an optimum time when it needs to be dealt with within our developmental stages. If the basic need is not met during this optimum time, it will be more difficult to meet later.

Third, *the longer you put off completing the psychological task of a particular stage, the harder it becomes ever to complete it.* This means that the longer we allow a specific psychological need to go unmet, the more it negatively affects psychological growth and development. The more it negatively affects psychological growth and development, the harder it becomes to go back and meet that need and, thereby, restore positive psychological health. In terms of the habits that people learn, we find this same principle to be true. The longer that a person continues a habit that might be detrimental to them, like addiction to cigaretttes, the harder it becomes to break that habit. In the same way, the longer an adolescent continues in aggressive delinquent behavior due to low self-esteem and lack of acceptance, the harder it becomes to change this child's behavior. The conclusion that we are making is that the longer that we continue in a particular psychological state, the harder it will be to ever break out of that state, even if it is negative and the person wants to change.

Fourth, *when the psychological task of one stage is not completed, it negatively affects the completion of the psychological tasks of all of the following stages*. The result is that when one psychological need in the hierarchy of basic human needs is not met, it becomes impossible to meet any of the following needs totally. This means that until you go back and finish the task associated with the first need in the hierarchy that was not completed, you cannot finish any of the stages that follow it. Through this assumption we can now understand why some people have more serious psychological problems than others. One of the primary components of psychopathology is the developmental background within which the person grew up. The more negative the background, the less the basic psychological needs were met, and the more likely that person will have serious psychological problems.

Implications for Counseling

We can now make three points related to our concern for people's psychological well being.

1. The question sometimes arises as to whether and when parents should seek outside help. The answer to this question is *the sooner the better*. We must change our view of counseling as a negative to counseling as a positive. If a basic psychological need in a child is not being met, we need to help the parents to stop focusing on themselves—in terms of blame—and to start focusing more on the well-being of the child. Too many parents resist seeking professional advice or aid for

their children's developmental problems. This will only lead to the problem becoming worse. Psychological and behavioral problems do not go away with time but only become more serious. Parents must be helped to see that their child's needs must come before their pride. The professional teacher, guidance counselor, and child psychologist are not there to make moral judgments on the parents but to help the child. Some parents may be reluctant to seek advice because they are not sure whether or not the problem is really serious. These parents are worried about looking foolish. Again professionals are there to answer questions. It is better to check out something and find out that it was not serious than not to check it out and later find out that it was.

2. The same principles hold true for adults. If a you are unhappy with life and seem to be going in circles, seek out counsel immediately. *Problems of psychological growth do not just go away, but can only get worse if we do not face them.* The professional counselor is there to help you, not to condemn or laugh at you. In adulthood the older you get, the more rigid you become. To put off dealing with psychological conflicts as a young adult merely leads to a life filled with greater psychological pain and suffering. There is a reason stemming from the developmental process why a person is experiencing psychological conflict. *Your problems make sense and they can be solved.* The message of Christianity and of Christian counseling is that through God there is always hope, since through God there is always the potential for a changed life.

3. *There is no need to live in the negative.* Today far too much of our time spent in Christian counseling, as well as counseling in general, is in the negative mode. People wait until their problems seem almost hopeless before they are willing to seek help. In terms of an analogy, we need to start spending more time on fire prevention than on putting out fires. The reason for this is that you can put out a fire and still lose the house. How much better it would be to keep the house from catching fire in the first place. The church needs to put a much greater emphasis on building good marriages rather than just saving sick ones. We need to focus much more upon how to turn the Christian body into a therapeutic community of wholeness. The value of Christian theories in psychology and more specifically this Christian theory of human development is that they should be able to allow us to move much more to a positive approach to Christian psychological health. To know what to do and when to do it in the development sequence allows us to prevent psychological problems more effectively from ever starting. Just as it was in medicine, the greatest advancement will be made in positive mental health when we can learn to prevent the problems from developing beyond their initial stages.

MATURATION AND LEARNING

Maturation

Maturation can be defined as the process within the developmental sequence of a person going from stage to stage at a defined or given rate of speed. As has already been discussed, the rate of maturation *places distinct limits upon what a child or an adult can learn or understand in relation to their psychological development at any given point in time*. To understand a person's rate of maturation is to understand what stage of development they should be in and the basic psychological need that must be met. Especially in terms of children, we need to view the maturation process as a friend rather than an enemy. Rather than to try and go against it, there is a great need to work within the developmental process as we raise and educate our children.

One of the problems in our society is that children who seem to have special abilities or talents are wrongly valued more highly than those who do not have these attributes. As a result, down deep most parents would like their children to be special; to be better than other children. These parental fantasies sometimes lead to a loss of objectivity on the part of the parents when they are dealing with their children, causing many parents to want their children to be advanced in their development, with only a few children who actually are.

The concept of comparing children as to their psychological maturation is done on the basis of a statistical distribution called the normal or bell-shaped curve, which was discussed earlier. When using this distribution we find that the attributes and abilities of people distribute themselves in such a way that most people end up in the middle. This means that most children mature according to the rule. Those children who in a particular area of development mature either slower than the norm or faster than the norm still do so within a pattern that is predictable. The slower maturing child at one stage will also mature slowly at the next. The faster maturing child at one stage will also be faster maturing at the next one.

One problem that arises, however, which many parents are not aware of or do not understand, is that human development has several components. This book is only concerned with the psychospiritual development of human beings; however, there are other areas in which development takes place. We must acknowledge here that a person also develops physically, cognitively, morally, and socially. Too often parents assume that because their child is advanced in one area of development, or has special gifts or abilities, the child also is advanced in other areas. There are certain areas of development—social and emotional development especially—in which almost all children progress at the same rate. It is in these areas that children suffer when parents place too much emphasis on some ability that brings the child a lot of social attention.

On the other hand, some children progress more slowly than others in certain areas of development. For example, the mentally retarded child progresses at a rate of maturation in the area of cognitive development that is slower than most other children. Sadly, too many times this child needlessly must suffer psychologically in relation to parents and peers because of this mental handicap. In the same way that we place too much value on gifted children, the society we live in today places too little value on children who are handicapped or different in some way. We must inform parents and society that the mentally retarded child has the same social and psychological needs that all children have. The retarded child who has emotional problems has them because of mistreatment, not because he or she is retarded. As Christians, we need to teach the world that in God's eyes all people have equal spiritual worth and value regardless of their earthly talents and abilities.

Maturation is a useful concept, therefore, in that it allows us to identify and meet the primary needs of people more fully. As we identify the maturational rate of a specific person, we can know what that person needs to be focusing on in terms of learning. By understanding a person's rate of maturation, we can then discuss that person's readiness to learn different things and deal with specific psychological tasks. Maturation tied to the developmental sequence creates for each individual a potential for experiencing and learning. For us to ask or force a child or adult to learn something before he or she is ready to learn, or has the potential to learn, only creates the opportunity for that person to fail. The byproduct of this experience of failure is a lowering of self-esteem and the beginning of psychological conflict.

Learning

Although important, maturation is not enough for a person to achieve psychological health. Maturation as a readiness to learn is still meaningless unless there is an opportunity for actual learning to take place. For a person to have the potential of experiencing the meeting of a specific psychological need because he or she is in a specific development stage is not enough. *Positive psychological growth cannot take place unless the person has the right environment and the right opportunities.* Again, especially as children, we do not always get to choose the environment within which we are living. Neither do we always get to choose those people who can affect our lives. As a result, no two people ever have exactly the same learning experiences and no two people are ever exactly alike psychologically. Since the learning experiences of each person differ, the types of experiences we have impact greatly upon who we are.

There are two basic directions in which the learning experiences of life can take us. The first is positive. Through learning we can grow, we can know, and our lives can be enriched. Through learning we can go places and meet people. Through learning we can develop skills and reach our goals. No one ever was born as an expert on anything other than crying, eating, and sleeping. Although everyone is born with a positive potential, that potential must be cultivated if it ever is to be fulfilled. This leads to the negative direction of learning. Through learning people can become mistrustful of others. Through learning people can become afraid of life. Through learning people can become addicted to drugs as an escape from problems. In other words, learning by itself is not automatically good. There are many things that can be learned in life that are harmful to us. We can be confronted with many experiences that will hurt us psychologically.

Within the developmental stages, therefore, we must be concerned not only with the specific need that must met, but also with establishing the right environment for the fulfilling of that need. Positive psychological growth requires, therefore, that we understand both the concept of maturation and the concept of learning. It is necessary to know both the psychological need that is in ascendency and the right climate needed to fulfill it.

Implications for Parenting

The understanding of the two concepts of maturation and learning become very important for parents in order to raise children positively. Good parenting is based upon the parents' identification of a true need in their child and then their provision of an environment where that need can be met. One of the goals of this book is to help parents in the task of parenting. There seem to be two major ways that parents can create problems for their children and for themselves. The first is through a lack of understanding of the importance of the concept of maturation. Maturation places limits on the child. *Some parents do not understand this and attempt to push their children too far too fast.* Although the child may be gifted in one area, he or she will probably not be progressing equally fast in other areas. As a result, the child experiences expectations and pressures that eventually become more than he or she can handle. Psychological problems are the result.

On the other hand, because *some parents do not understand the impor-*

tance of learning, they socially, educationally, psychologically, and spiritually deprive the child. It is one thing for children not to learn something because it is beyond their capabilities; it is another not to learn it because they never had a chance. We need to encourage parents to see themselves as teachers and trainers of their children. We need to help parents to become actively involved in the learning process of their children. Too much of what our children learn today is outside of our control because we, as parents, have chosen to not be involved. We have turned over learning to the TV set. We have turned over learning to the school. We have turned over learning to the peer group. One of the reasons why so many of our young people are confused and lost today is because of their parents' inability to teach them the purpose and meaning of life. We need more parents who are willing to be teachers of their children and show them the way that they should go.

3

Innocence Stage

Our first psychospiritual stage of human development is the Innocence Stage. This stage involves the baby in the womb of the mother and runs from conception to birth. In terms of the Biblical eras, the Innocence Stage corresponds with Adam and Eve in the Garden of Eden. Without any knowledge of evil and in perfect fellowship with God, before the fall Adam and Eve were in a state of innocence, living in their perfect environment with all of their needs being met. In the same way, the baby lives in the mother's womb, deriving life-sustaining food and oxygen from the mother through the umbilical cord. Protected from the harsh outer world by the protective environment in which it lives, the baby is surrounded by amniotic fluid which keeps the temperature around the body constant and protects the child from physical harm. The mother and child are wondrously intertwined together as one flesh within the perfect plan of God's creation.

The processes by which a sperm and an egg unite and eventually transform themselves into a new living human being are so complicated and so detailed that it becomes very difficult to understand how anyone could actually believe that the human race came about by chance or by accident. And yet, many people today still view the beginning of life as simply a biological process developed over millions of years through some evolutionary sequence. By establishing a relationship between the Innocence Stage and Garden of Eden, we are attacking this secular humanistic explanation as to the origin of man. The major premise of this book is that man began as a miraculous creation of God and that the developmental process that all men go through was established by God, and not by human evolution. In this chapter we are taking the further stand that each new life, each new baby, also involves a creative, supernatural act of God. This means that the newly conceived baby in a mother's womb is more than a biological life; it is also a spiritual life.

SPIRITUAL ORIGIN

Many Christians do not adequately understand the true meaning of the nature of man. The secular humanistic view is that man is only a biological organism and that life exists on a one-dimensional plane. The materialistic-monism view of man is based on the idea that man is just a body controlled by a brain who thinks, feels, and chooses because of totally explainable physiological processes and biochemical reactions. On this basis, as far as social scientists are concerned, man is just another animal evolved from animals. The uniqueness of man is said to be that of a more highly evolved brain. This means that the secular humanistic doctor or scientist views the newly conceived baby as only a biological organism. To them the life of that organism is merely a physical life; the same physical life that all animals have. As a result, they refer to this baby as a fetus or an embryo in the same way that a cow, a monkey, or a dog has a fetus. To the secular humanist, life is only physical: In the process of human development, man is reduced to an animal and the value of this new life is reduced to its biological value. Because biological life comes only from "dust" through an accidental process of human evolution, its value is no more than "dust."

The Christian view of the beginning of life is different. The Christian concept of the nature of man is one of dualistic interactionism. The origin of man stemmed from a creation of God, not through evolution over millions of years. Genesis 2:7 states, "And the Lord God formed man of the dust of the ground and breathed into his nostrils the breath of life and man became a living soul." This passage teaches that there are two dimensions to human nature, not one. Man does have a physical dimension, a body, which comes from dust. However, man is much more than just a physical body; man is also a living soul. There is a spiritual dimension of human nature that goes beyond what scientists can see with microscopes or record on machines. This spiritual dimension, breathed into man by God, makes man unique. This means that man is more than an animal since he is more than a body. The spiritual dimension is unique only to man, as established in Genesis 1:27. "So God created man in His own image, in the image of God created He him; male and female created He them." As we discuss the origin of life, then, we must include man's spirit as well as his body.

For too long we have allowed the debate over the moral implications of abortion to center only on the question of the origin of physical life. As Christians, we have been on the defensive because we have not established a presuppositional base for our efforts. As a result, the debate has centered largely upon the question of when life begins, with no distinction being made as to our definition of life. The Christian must be made aware that the debate over abortion arises from a difference of opinion over the definition concerning the nature of man. In this way, we can see that the debate is not a scientific debate over the origin of life controlled by scientists armed with scientific facts. Instead, the debate concerning whether abortion is right or wrong actually stems from a philosophical disagreement over the structure of human nature. This makes the debate not one of facts versus facts—or one of facts versus faith—but one of faith versus faith. The abortion issue leads us back to the same two antagonists that are fighting for control of our society—secular humanism and Christianity. In this battle Christianity is attempting to defend the value of human life because of its unique creation from the point of conception. On the other hand, secular humanism denies the spiritual dimension of man, the existence of God, and turns the early months of life into only a biological process to be studied scientifically. From this perspective, a baby becomes merely its atoms, molecules, and cells, and the infant's value is questioned.

The Christian position then is that man has both a spirit and a body. The spirit of man is that which makes him unique, and this spirit stems from God, not human evolution. When does the spirit come to be be joined to the body? The creative act of God where the dust and the spirit are brought together takes place at the point of conception. In this way, the fertilization of the sperm of the father and the egg of the mother merely create a new human body. At the same time that the baby is created physically by the parents, God breathes its spirit into it and it becomes a living soul. This means that God is as much the parent of each new life as the mother and father are. Since it is the spirit given by God that makes the child unique, each baby actually belongs more to God than it does to the parents. God then has a vested interest in each new life, and anything we do as humans to that life will eventually need to be accounted for before God. The issue of life and the taking of life through abortion must be evaluated on the basis of God's word and God's truth, not human reasoning. Scientists are not God and neither are medical doctors. This is neither a scientific nor a medical question; it is a spiritual question and God's word must prevail.

BIBLICAL BASE

The first question that an interested Christian might ask would be, Is there support to the previously stated position that spiritual life begins before physical birth? In the past many Christians believed that only physical life begins at conception—the child does not become a spiritual being until the time of physical birth, when the baby leaves the womb of the mother. We rejected this argument because of our Biblical stages of human development. The baby in the womb of the mother is a spiritual life as well as a physical one, because Adam and Eve in the

Garden of Eden were not animals but specific spiritual creations of God. Therefore, the first basis for saying that abortion is murder is theoretical.

Our second reason is Biblical. The Bible supports our theoretical stand in specific passages that clearly indicate the truth that a baby in the womb is spiritually as well as physically alive. Four Biblical references support our conclusion. The first is found in Isaiah 49:1, where it states, "The Lord hath called me from the womb; from the bowels of my mother has he made mention of my name." Also, in Luke 1:44 the spiritual existence of the child in the womb is substantiated. "For lo as soon as the voice of thy salvation sounded in mine ears, the babe leaped in my womb for joy." It is in Psalm 139:13-16 where we can establish that God is involved supernaturally in the creation of each individual life:

> For Thou didst form my inward parts; Thou didst weave me in my mother's womb. I will give thanks to Thee for I am fearfully and wonderfully made; wonderful are Thy works, and my soul knows it very well. My frame was not hidden from Thee, when I was made in secret, and skillfully wrought in the depths of the earth. Thine eyes have seen my unformed substance; and in Thy book they were all written the days that were ordained for me when as yet there was not one of them.
>
> *(New American Standard Version)*

This passage establishes not only the omnipotence of God but also His omniscience. The final passage that establishes God's involvement in the creative process, in terms of the beginning of each new life, is Jeremiah 1:5: "Before I formed thee in the womb I knew thee and before thou came forth out of the womb I sanctified thee."

All of these passages clearly lead the Christian who believes the Bible to be the inspired Word of God to the conclusion that spiritual life does begin before physical birth. These passages support both of our original statements. First, God is creatively involved in the beginning of each new life by giving it a spirit that exists in interrelationship with the body created by the human parents. It is only through the merging of this body and spirit that man becomes a living soul. Second, the Bible supports the idea that the beginning of man as a living soul is not at physical birth, but earlier—while the baby is in the womb of the mother. As implied in these Scriptures, the most logical time to place this merger of the two parts of man is at the point of conception.

PSYCHOLOGICAL ORIGIN

The psychological origin of the baby also begins at conception. From the first days of life the baby is not only growing physically, it is also growing psychologically. The baby in the womb is truly alive in the sense that it can interact with its world. Scientists have been able to show that as early as six weeks after conception the baby can be conditioned to respond to a specific stimulus. This means that the baby is capable of learning at least as early as one and a half months after conception, and possibly earlier. This is well before the time when most abortions take place.

Babies are also psychologically living beings in that they are capable of emotionally interacting with their environment. Research data has been collected over the last decade supporting the idea that the psychological states of the mother during pregnancy can have a direct influence on the baby while still in the womb. One example reveals the story of a seventeen-year-old girl who gave birth to an apparently healthy baby boy. Twenty hours later, however, the baby began to vomit fresh blood and continued to do so for one hour until he died. The post-mortem examination revealed three peptic ulcers, something usually found in adults who are chronically tense and anxious. The connection here was one that the psychological stress of the mother was able to affect directly the well-being of the baby. In a follow-up case history, it was found that the teenage girl was indeed under a great deal of stress. Coerced by her parents into getting married to the father of the baby, she found herself during pregnancy living with an alcoholic husband who physically abused her. Although she left him during pregnancy, he continued to harass her and the day before delivery threw a brick through her bedroom window, causing her severe emotional turmoil.

The research evidence being gathered today within psychology all points to the conclusion that the temperament differences found in babies at birth can best be accounted for by the emotional learning of the baby during pregnancy. The old view being discarded is that these differences in temperament are primarily caused by genetics; which means that they are inborn. In terms of the nature/nurture controversy, most of the differences in temperament among babies at birth can now be attributed to psychological states of the mother during pregnancy.

Four variables have been found to be most relevant to the psychological well-being of the baby at birth: 1) the woman's psychological functioning, including her relationship to her mother; 2) the woman's state of physical health and physical habits; 3) the emotional climate present in the marriage between the husband and wife; and 4) the sociocultural milieu of the couple. For the purposes of attempting to establish the prenatal origin of the baby as a psychological being, the most astounding finding is that it is the first trimester of pregnancy that correlates most with post-partum adaptation of the baby. Most related to post-partum differences in temperament are the mother's psychological health and marital happiness early in pregnancy. For example, recent research has found a strong relationship between the anxiety and depression level of mothers during the third month of pregnancy and the irritability of their babies at birth.

The present focus on natural childbirth using Lamaze techniques and on establishing a positive atmosphere in the delivery room as established by Frederick LeBoyer also assumes that the child is already a psychological living being when it is born. The behavioristic view that the child begins as a blank slate at birth cannot be supported. All of the evidence seems to point to the fact that the psychological origin of the baby begins in the womb, not at the point of physical birth. From conception, the baby is a living psychological being in that it is capable of thinking and feeling and, therefore, may be affected emotionally while still in the womb. Beyond the theoretical and Biblical evidence that the baby in the womb is spiritually alive, we can now add the psychological evidence that the act of abortion is more than just the termination of a physical organism. Abortion involves the termination of a living human soul, and this is murder.

HUMAN RESPONSIBILITY

We have now established that the psychospiritual development of each new life begins at the point of conception. This stage of life from the point of conception to the point of birth was called the Innocence Stage because the baby is totally innocent to its environment and its fate. The baby does not interact directly with its mother in terms of free will and is not allowed to have any voice in its fate. It neither chose to be conceived nor had any voice in who would be its parents. The baby does not choose to eat, choose to breathe, or choose to sleep. Instead, it is totally dependent upon its mother for life, both physically and psychologically.

At this point, both the physical and psychological well-being of the baby are totally within the hands of its mother. This means that God has given the *Mother* primary responsibility for her baby and this responsibility begins at conception, not at birth. The major task of mothering is twofold and relates to the meeting of the baby's basic physical and psychological needs. Most mothers are aware that they must directly meet their child's physical and psychological needs after birth, but we have largely failed to educate mothers of newly conceived babies that they can have just as strong an impact on the physical and psychological health of the child before he or she is born. The reason that we have neglected the development of the baby before birth is that there was no feedback system to indicate its importance. The major view of medical and psychological experts in the past was that the process of development during pregnancy was pre-determined. This meant that the mother was led to believe that pregnancy was merely a biological condition or state. We now need to inform mothers that pregnancy is also a time for psychospiritual development and that they are responsible.

The first area of responsibility of the mother is in meeting the child's physical needs. Mothers need to understand that they start feeding the baby the minute it is conceived. Before birth the mother feeds the baby by feeding herself. This means that proper nutrition for the baby's health is determined by the kinds of food the mother eats. What she eats is only one way that the mother is able to physically affect her baby. She needs to get adequate rest and sleep and to keep herself from getting overly fatigued. To the extent that she does not do this her baby is negatively affected. The mother also needs to get exercise and keep herself in good physical condition. Overall, as the mother is physically healthier, the baby will be physically healthier both before and after birth. Finally, the mother must be aware that the drugs she puts into her body and bloodstream have the capacity to negatively affect her baby. The main focus here must be on the millions of women who drink alcohol, smoke cigarettes and marijuana, and take the various pills available among teenagers and young adults. Many of these women do not understand that everything which enters their bodies also enters the body of their baby. It is one thing to pollute your own body against the will of God through the use of alcohol and drugs, but it is another to pollute the body of an innocent baby who has no choice in the matter. Today babies are being born who are already drug addicts and alcoholics. Mothers need to see that they are accountable to God for what they do to their babies while they are pregnant through the way they take care of themselves physically.

A mother's second area of responsibility during pregnancy is in meeting the psychological needs of her baby. The most basic psychological need of the baby in the womb is to have a mother who has a positive self-concept or self-esteem. The emotional climate during pregnancy is established by the mother's view of herself, not her view of the baby. As the mother feels positive about life, about her marriage, and about pregnancy, she will begin to establish a positive bond with the life inside her long before she ever sees it or even senses its presence. Mothers who are happy with living are happy with the life living inside them. This is the primary reason we must reject the idea that the mother who chooses to abort her baby does so for positive psychological reasons. Mothers who choose to obtain abortions do so because of too little self-esteem, not too much. An added problem is that the act of abortion as a violation of life and conscience only serves to lower the self-esteem of those who have very little positive self-love in the first place. It is hard to believe that women will ever find liberation by physically and psychologically abusing their unborn babies as they physically and psychologically abuse themselves. This is not freedom or liberation, but slavery. Women will only obtain true liberation by returning to God's teachings concerning the sanctity of motherhood and the value of human life, including that of unborn babies.

Women who want to have babies must go one step farther. They must see that the psychological health of the baby begins while still in the womb, through the psychological state of the mother during pregnancy. Tension, stress, depression, anxiety, fear, and anger all can have an effect upon the baby's emotional development. The mother must be taught that her emotional moods and states all involve corresponding physiological changes in her body which are then transferred to her unborn child. In the same way that a positive outlook on life leads to positive temperament development, a negative outlook and negative emotional states affect the development of a child's temperament in a negative way.

This leads us to the father's responsibility to the needs of the unborn baby. Since many of the negative moods or emotional states of the mother are a direct result of conflict with the father, he is also involved in the psychospiritual development of the baby during the Innocence Stage. The father must work to establish a positive emotional climate during pregnancy and build up his wife's self-esteem. In doing this, he is not only meeting his wife's needs, he is also helping to meet the psychological needs of his unborn child. Also, the father must spend just as much time establishing a positive climate in the early months of pregnancy as in the latter. Too many fathers only make an effort to be nicer to their wife and help her out at the end of pregnancy. Instead, the father needs to be involved from the beginning.

GOD'S JUDGMENT

The message of God's judgment is based on the fact that He gave man a free will. Through this free will man is allowed to choose. All choices, however, are not equally good and God uses His word to instruct us as to how we are to live. From this free will that we have been given comes responsibility. If we make a free choice, we become responsible for the consequences of that choice. Eventually God steps back into this process of choice in that He holds us accountable for the choices we have made. In the end every person who has made free choices will come to be judged by God according to His standards of judgment. No one will escape. The Bible makes it perfectly clear that the wrath of God will eventually be kindled and released upon those who prey upon the innocent and helpless people in the world in making free choices.

Many people believe in women's rights, and one of these rights is the freedom to choose whether the baby developing within a woman should live or die. Many will argue that no one or no law should be allowed that restricts a woman's freedom of choice, and in this case the control over her own body. From God's perspective, He allows a woman to make the choice as to whether or not she will use birth control contraceptives. Finally, He allows her to choose whether or not she will kill her baby through an abortion. At the same time, however, God also holds her accountable for every choice she makes. For many women, the very reason they seek an abortion is because they previously freely chose to break other commandments of God concerning premarital sex and adultery. With God we do not solve the problem of one sin by committing another one to try to cover it up. In the Bible, David tried this and it did not work. Sin only can be resolved through confession and God's forgiveness.

As an individual decision, the blood of the dead baby will be on the mother's hands. She chose to kill it; she will stand accountable before God for her choice. However, the accountability goes well beyond the mother. The husband or boyfriend who got the woman pregnant, especially if done through immorality, also is involved by free choice. To the extent that he encourages or pressures her to get an abortion, God will hold him accountable also. This means that the blood of unborn babies killed through abortions will also be on the hands of the fathers who contributed to this action. But it does not stop there. The doctor who performed the abortion, whether Christian or not, also does so through free choice. No one forces the doctor to kill unborn babies. There are many doctors who are materially getting rich through the killing of unborn babies. Because they are involved in the deaths of many babies, the wrath of God will be unleashed the greatest on them. These doctors are mass executioners of life, the blood of unborn babies is on their hands, and they will not escape God's judgment.

But the responsibility does not stop with the doctors. In our society, it is legal within our system of laws for this practice of abortion to continue. Over one million unborn babies are killed each year in this country through choices of human free will. As a result, the whole nation has become involved in this holocaust. To the extent that Christians and Christian churches have been and are continuing to be silent, they will also be held accountable by God for their inaction. If this silence continues, the blood of the dead babies will be on the hands of Christians. What is worse even than the silence of many Christians is the active open support of abortion by others who call themselves Christians. How long can this abomination to God continue? How long will God let the cries and the blood of the deaths of innocent unborn babies go unpunished? Yes, sinful man does have the right to make free choices, but when these free choices come at the expense of others and attack the sanctity of life, God's wrath is kindled and His judgment is sure. As individuals and as a society, we must all repent and put a stop to this slaughter before it is too late. All true Christians under the Lordship of Christ must stand up now and challenge this act of destruction promoted by Satan in his attempts to gain control of our nation. Soon it will be too late.

4
Nurturance Stage

The Nurturance Stage begins at the point of physical birth and extends to around two years of age. In terms of our Biblical eras, this stage corresponds to the time period between Adam and Eve after leaving the Garden to the time of Noah and the flood. This means that through the birth process the baby leaves the state of innocence when it leaves the womb of the mother. As this newborn child enters the world of reality outside the protection of the womb, it finds immediately that survival is more difficult and life is more frustrating. The baby is now capable of interacting directly with the environment, and how the baby reacts affects the way that his or her needs are met. When the baby leaves the womb of the mother, it is forced to go from total dependency, in terms of life stemming from the umbilical cord, to total egocentrism, in terms of only being able to focus on his own immediate needs. The newborn has no ability to delay gratification. At this point this total egocentrism must be considered normal, as can be seen in the normal reaction of a baby crying when it is hungry. This state of total egocentrism of infancy is reflected in the Bible in Psalm 58:3: "The wicked are estranged from the womb: they go astray as soon as they are born, speaking lies." If not adequately dealt with, egocentrism can continue throughout life, as reflected in Genesis 6:5: "And God saw that the wickedness of man was great in the earth and that every imagination of the thoughts of his heart was only evil continually." This passage indicates that mankind before the time of Noah had progressed no further in its emotional development than the complete egocentrism we find in young infants during the Nurturance Stage. The conclusion is that in a state of complete egocentrism the new baby is capable of communicating when his or her needs remain unmet, but is totally incapable of meeting those needs by him- or herself. What every baby needs at this stage of life is a nurturing mother figure.

BIBLICAL BASE

The term *nurturance* centers around the idea of a mother loving, caring for, and meeting the needs of her baby. One concept found in the Bible that represents this stage is that of nursing. In Exodus 2:8,9 we read, "And the maid went and called the child's mother. And Pharoah's daughter said unto her, Take this child away and nurse it for me. And the woman took the child and nursed it." Also in Ruth 4:16 we find, "And Naomi took the child and laid it in her bosom, and became nurse unto it." In both of these passages nursing was associated with mothering the baby and seeking to meet its needs. Yet nursing and mothering a child include more than just meeting the physical needs. As stated at I Thessalonians 2:7, "But we were gentle among you even as a nurse cherisheth her children." In this passage we see that mothering includes a psychological dimension—the need of the child to be cherished by the mother. This psychological dimension of mothering is also reflected in Isaiah 66:12,13 in relation to the need for comfort. "Behold I will extend peace to her like a river . . . then shall you suck, you shall be born upon her sides and dangled upon her knees. As one whom his mother comforts, so will I comfort you."

The final important Biblical principle that needs to be discussed in this section concerns the suggested idea of a mothering instinct. Since mothering within the animal world is largely controlled through instinctual, predetermined factors, many people also think of human mothering as an innate instinct. In this view, all women are born with the desire to mother and by maternal instinct know how to mother. This idea is derived from a secular humanistic view that man is an animal evolved from animals. The woman as an evolved animal automatically by instinct knows how to love and nurture her baby. This is just not true. In humans, God gave a free will that animals do not have. As a result, the human mother must learn to mother and choose to mother. Many new mothers feel that something is wrong with them because, at the point of birth, they find themselves insecure and afraid about their ability to be a good mother. These mothers need to be told that the reason they feel uncertain about whether or not they will be a good mother is because good mothering is not automatic. To be a good mother requires that the mother choose to learn the psychological as well as physical needs of her baby and choose to do her best to meet those needs. The fact that not all mothers automatically are good mothers is found in Isaiah 49:15: "Can a woman forget her sucking child, that she should not have compassion on the son of her womb? Yea, they may forget, yet I will not forget thee." This passage affirms what we already know about human mothering—that it is possible for a mother to neglect, reject, and/or abuse her baby. Positive mothering, therefore, is not inevitable because of the fall of man and the sinful nature within each person.

HUMAN RESPONSIBILITY

The conclusion drawn from the above Biblical references is that God has given mankind the responsibility for nurturing and raising children. Also, because of the free will of man the fulfillment of this responsibility is something that must be chosen. As a result, it is possible for two people to create a baby that they do not want through the act of sexual intercourse. Although they consciously chose to have sex, at the same time they did not feel they were consciously choosing to have a baby. The phrase used by many people today is that the baby "was an accident." As discussed in the previous chapter, many people feel that if the baby started as an accident rather than a conscious choice, they are not responsible for what happens to the child.

This is not God's position. From God's perspective, to choose to have sexual intercourse implies a second choice—that of accepting the responsibilty of a baby that might result from that act. This is why God ordained marriage and told us that sex was to be reserved for marriage. In other words, under the plan of God the first purpose of human sexual activity is procreation, not pleasure. Today we live in a society where pleasure is separated from responsibility. Young people want to have the pleasure of sex without being willing to accept the responsibilities of parenthood. God teaches us in His word that true happiness in life only comes through the fulfillment of our responsibilities, not the running away from them. The baby neither chooses to be conceived, nor chooses its parents. It is totally helpless without the nurturance of a mother who is willing to choose to take care of it.

Primary Responsibility

The primary responsibility of the Nurturance Stage has been given by God to the *Mother*. This does not mean that the father has no responsibility to the child during the first two years of life. God has given a secondary responsibility for the nurturance of the child to the father. Any father who steps in and tries to instruct his wife on how to nurture a baby is overstepping his boundaries and is outside the will of God. The father should take his cues from the mother and think of himself as a support person. He should begin this support of the mother from the minute the wife knows she is pregnant. The father should be involved in the process of birth by standing by his wife and encouraging her during labor, so that he can celebrate with her the miracle of life when the child is born. In the same way that the mother establishes a bond with her baby during pregnancy and birth, the father also needs to establish an emotional bond with the child as soon as possible after he or she is born. During the early years of life, the father needs to continue to be supportive of his wife and spend time with his child. When the mother is tired, the father can do things around the house or watch the child or change the diapers. If the mother needs to get away for an evening, the father should be able to step in and run the household. In other words, whenever the mother says "help" the father should be there to pitch in and help out. In this way, the father from the very beginning gets to know his child, is drawn closer to his wife, and truly begins to build a family.

Still, the father is not to replace the mother or even be an equal with her. God created mothers to be mothers. God gave the mother the primary responsibility for meeting her baby's needs from the time of conception throughout most of early childhood. It is the mother that God will hold accountable if the baby's needs are not met. Mothers are responsible for protecting their babies from harm and providing them with love and affection. This means that God's judgment will come down upon any mother who rejects, neglects, or abuses her baby. This mother would be better off to put the baby up for adoption, so that the baby's need for nurturance can be met, than to try and raise it while she herself is still too emotionally immature to do it adequately. In terms of society as a whole, women must accept their responsibility to protect the rights and needs of helpless babies. If we ever reach the point at which women no longer care about the hurts and sufferings of young children inflicted by immature and neurotic parents, we are doomed. Who will save the children when we reach the point at which mothers' hearts become hardened to the cries of their own babies?

Major Task

The major task of the mother during the Nurturance Stage is to meet the basic physical and psychological needs of the newborn infant. Without a mother to feed it, the baby would die of starvation. Without a mother to clothe it, the baby would die of exposure. Without a mother to love it, the baby would die of a broken heart. Most mothers are generally aware of the basic physical needs of the infant, and within our society unmet physical needs are not usually the problem. Although it still occurs throughout the world, very few babies in this country die of physical starvation or deprivation. What many mothers are not aware of, especially the immature teenagers who become parents, is that the mothering responsibility is a psychological one as well. Psychological neglect and deprivation arise when women who become mothers have never experienced the meeting of their own psychological needs. In other words, it is hard for a mother who does not have enough food to feed herself to produce enough milk at her breast to feed her baby. In the same way, a mother who had never experienced love as a child will find it impossible to give love on a lasting basis to her child. This means that no mother will be able to meet the basic psychological needs of her children adequately until she has been able to meet her own successfully. This is why many mothers feels so insecure and guilty about their mothering—they know they do not really love their baby, primarily because they have no love to give.

The initial bond of the baby is with its mother, and it is to this mother that the baby looks for the meeting of his or her basic psychological and physical needs. This early attachment to the mother is supported in psychological research. Experiments have been conducted to study the effects of day-care experience on the mother-infant bond. One research found that despite the fact that day-care children probably spent more of their waking hours at the center than at home, the day-care experience did nothing to alter the children's overwhelming preference for their mothers when they were bored or apprehensive. This finding is confirmed by another study on kibbutz-reared children in Israel who spent more than twenty hours a day in an infant house. These children still showed a strong preference for their own mothers.

Other research has compared children from nontraditional families with children from traditional families. The nontraditional group included people from communal living, social contract marriages, and single mothers (by choice rather than divorce or separation). The findings were that children from nontraditional families differed very little from those raised in traditional families. The way that both groups of children were brought up was largely the same. In all groups it was the mother who was the primary caretaker of the child.

Other researchers have investigated how the experiences of the first years of life contribute to the positive development of the child. The conclusion was that the origins of human competence are to be found in what turned out to be the most critical time of life—between six months and two years. The child's experiences during this period do more to determine future psychological, social, and educational competence than at any other time that follows. Researchers started by defining those attributes associated with competent children at age six and then investigating when these skills developed. They found that the youngest children in their sample, who were barely three, already possessed the social and intellectual skills that distinguished the outstanding six year olds. This meant that these abilities were already established before three. Over a period of time, the research team eventually established data to show that patterns of experience and reaction of children at twelve and fifteen months can be correlated with achievements of general competence at three. The single, most important environmental factor contributing to the differences among the children was found to be the mother and the quality of her mothering. The children who developed best had almost twice as much social interaction with their mother as those who had more problems in development.

It has been found that the best mothers excel in three key areas. First, they are good designers and organizers of their child's environment. In other words, good mothers take an active approach to mothering rather than a passive one. Good mothers think of themselves as teachers of their children, not just babysitters. Second, good mothers are firm in establishing guidelines for their children while simultaneously showing great affection and love. These mothers are not afraid to set limits for their children and establish boundaries on dependency. At the same time, these mothers are not afraid of their emotions and being close. Finally, good mothers serve as personal consultants to their children in brief episodes of less than one minute. The child is encouraged to explore and initiate play. These mothers allow the child to decide when they need to move close to the mother or move away from the mother. During closeness, this mother focuses her attention responsively to the child. The conclusion, therefore, from developmental research is that the mother is essential during the Nurturance Stage for positive psychological development.

Major Technique

The major technique through which the mother is to meet the basic physical and psychological needs of her young child is *Unconditional Nurturance*. More than a technique, unconditional nurturance is really an attitude. This attitude is associated with giving love rather than getting love. Unconditional nurturance is the mother's willingness to give love to her baby without expecting the baby to give it back in return. As established earlier in this chapter, the baby is completely egocentric, which means that it is incapable of giving love. The baby can only take. Many young immature women have babies in a state of love deprivation with the hope that their need for love will be met by the baby. In reality, babies do not and cannot love; initially they only frustrate. The baby's demands on the mother are continuous and insatiable, and the burden of mothering, as established in the curse (Genesis 3:16), can become hard to bear. Eventually, the frustration in the mother can build up to the point where the impulse can come to hurt her child or run away from him or her. In this state the mother, who had a baby to obtain more love for herself, feels guilty about these negative feelings toward her baby, with the result that she loves herself less.

Unconditional nurturance can only stem from a heart full of love, not one seeking love. Mothers who are still seeking love through the baby will begin to place conditions upon their mothering. This mother is only willing to nurture and love if the baby fulfills certain requirements or meets certain needs of the mother. This is called conditional nurturance. When the baby does not do this, the mother can retaliate through neglect and/or abuse. Either way, the child suffers. On the other hand, the good mother is able to give freely of her love to the baby without initial expectations of return. Nurturance is not a weapon to be used, but a responsibility to be fulfilled.

Focal Point

The focal point for the unconditional nurturance of the young infant and the meeting of the baby's first psychological need in our hierarchy is *body contact*. On the physical level, the baby needs a mother who is willing to clothe it, feed it, change its diapers, and assure that it gets enough sleep. On the psychospiritual level, the baby needs to be touched. God created humans with a need for social interaction, and this need begins at birth. For proper psychological development, the newborn infant needs to be talked to, looked at, played with, and cuddled. It is through this touching and social interaction that the baby is able to distinguish itself as an individual and to feel loved. During the first months of life one of the best times for this important social interaction is during and after feeding. The baby is most alert for social stimulation during this time. This means that more important than whether a mother breast feeds or bottle feeds her baby is the positive attention and body contact she gives the child during the process.

Goal of Stage

In summary we now have established that the primary responsibility for the Nurturance Stage is placed by God upon the mother. She is responsible for meeting the child's basic physical and psychological needs. The technique used is one of unconditional nurturance, where the psychological need to be loved is met primarily through body contact and social interaction. Through this process the goal of the Nurturance Stage can be reached, which is that the child eventually comes *to feel safe within the arms of its mother's love*. The infant's world will be viewed as threatening, but the child should feel like there is a place to which he or she can retreat. A hurt child runs to mother, a frightened child runs to mother, an excited child runs to mother. And in all cases the good mother listens and comforts. The safety of mother is essential to the child's development. No matter what the child faces in life, it is easier to bear if he or she knows that his or her mother is always there waiting as a refuge and shelter in the time of storm. The loving mother bandages the wounds, consoles the child, and then encourages him or her to try again, without ridicule, judgment, or criticism. In doing this, the mother creates a place of safety for her child.

PSYCHOLOGICAL NEED

Basic Need

The basic need associated with the Nurturance Stage is to develop in the child a sense of *security*. Security includes confidence that basic physical needs will be met. Security also includes confidence that basic psychological needs for body contact and social interaction will be met. Finally, security includes confidence that whenever the world seems too threatening a retreat can be made back to mother's arms and she will make the child feel safe again. The mother cannot demonstrate her love for her child through the use of words, since to a baby words are meaningless. Instead, the mother demonstrates her love for her baby through unconditional nurturance and the positive emotional climate she establishes. To the extent that the baby feels secure in the environment, he or she will feel loved and wanted. To the extent that the baby feels insecure because important needs are not being met, he or she will feel unloved and rejected. Security, therefore, stems from the idea that someone cares for us, wants to meet our needs, and is willing to protect us from harm. The resultant positive emotional state that arises in the child when the need for security has been met is *Peace*. In the baby peace usually follows a full tummy and some play with mommy. In most cases, the result is that the child falls asleep. Peace and contentment are, therefore, associated with happy children who feel secure and safe because they feel they have a loving mother who will take care of them.

Psychological State

During the Innocence Stage, the psychological state was one of total dependency. The unborn baby was tied directly to the mother through the umbilical cord on which he was totally dependent for life. In the

Nurturance Stage, through the process of birth, the child separates from the mother and becomes autonomous. Still this self cannot survive on its own. It remains dependent on its mother for the meeting of its needs. However, it is no longer totally dependent upon its mother for stimulation and learning. Eventually the child becomes mobile; first through crawling and then through walking. Through this mobility, the child is able on his or her own to move away from and toward mother. This process is called exploration, and it is very important to the child's intellectual and psychological development. The psychological state that best allows the child to explore in a positive way is *sheltered dependence*. Sheltered dependence allows the child to explore within safe limits and the continued protection of his or her mother. A mother who tries to keep her child in a state of total dependency will overprotect the child and block his or her growth and development. On the other hand, a mother who allows the child too much freedom and autonomy in its exploration runs the risk of having the child get hurt. The good mother finds a positive balance between freedom and control.

Self-Esteem

Through positive mothering in the Nurturance Stage, the child is able to build a positive sense of self. This sense of positive worth is called self-esteem. In this stage self-esteem centers around the idea of being *special*. The child feels special when its needs are met by a loving mother through unconditional nurturance. To the extent that the mother uses conditional nurturance, however, the child will not feel special. The idea of specialness, therefore, is based on a child's belief that he or she does not have to earn it. *I am special just because I exist. I have worth and value just because I am the child of my parents and no matter what I do I will never lose this.*

It is important that the parents do not tie the child's sense of being special into the child's performance, especially as the child gets older. The parents also should refrain from tying the sense of being special to the child's sex, abilities, or place in the birth order. As Christians, we also need to convey to our children that they are special because God helped make them and He loves them too.

It would be nice if we could just stop with the positive side of mothering and the Nurturance Stage and every child could have positive self-esteem. The problem is that this does not fit reality. The humanistic view holds to man's innate goodness, that children unhampered by social restrictions have an innate good potential that can be actualized. As Christians, we also believe that each person is created in the image of God with a potential for good. We also seek to help each child actualize within the potential God has given him or her. On the other hand, we believe the Bible when it discusses the fall of man and the reality of sin. Children at birth, therefore, not only have a potential for good, but also have a sinful nature and a potential for evil. This means that the conflict over human development is not only between the child and his or her environment but also between the good and evil that exists within each child from birth. We must disagree, therefore, with humanistic psychologists who say that it is possible to raise a child free from sin and free from evil. Since the fall of man, marred psychospiritual development is inevitable. This means that no child can be raised perfectly and no child can be raised without psychological and physical pain.

The curse on the mother associated with mothering is that she wants to nurture perfectly. She wants to mother her child in such a way that the child never hurts. But this is an impossibility. She cannot prevent hurt; she can only help her child to deal with it. Because of the fall there is sin, and because of sin there is hurt. A mother needs to accept this reality in her life and the life of her children. There are three areas in which sin is present, making the psychological marring of the child inevitable. First, there is sin in the environment. Everywhere the young child turns there is potential danger; in the medicine cabinet, under the sink, on the stairs, in the street. It is impossible for the mother to be everywhere, especially if she has more than one child. Eventually the environment will hurt all her children. Second, there is sin in the parents. Even if the mother could protect the child totally from a hostile world, she still would not be able to protect the child from a hostile self. No parent can parent perfectly, because no parent is perfect. In our humanity as parents we make mistakes, we get angry, we yell at our children, we criticize them. All of this is sin, and it negatively affects our children. Finally, there is sin in the child. The sin of the child is not just a byproduct of his or her sinful environment and sinful parents. There is a sinful nature within each child. At birth a child is completely egocentric, seeking to go his or her own way. Therefore, even if we could place our child in a perfect environment and operate perfectly as parents, which we cannot, we still could not prevent our child from experiencing negative psychological states and emotions. Sin then is inevitable in every child, and its effects must be expected and eventually faced.

Negative Cognitive States

There are two basic negative cognitive states that stem from inadequate nurturance. As just discussed, these states are inevitable in every child no matter how good a job the mother does. The quality of the mother's nurturance, however, does affect how deeply these states root themselves in the child's life; so it is important for the mother to try to do her best. The cognitive state the child experiences when all of his or her needs are not met with immediate gratification is one of *deprivation*. The negative emotional state associated with deprivation is *frustration*. The problem for the mother is that some of the baby's needs are contradictory in that they compete with each other. In other words, as the mother is meeting one need, she is delaying the meeting of another. As a result, all children will experience the cognitive state of deprivation and the negative emotional state of frustration.

The second negative cognitive state is experienced when the mother/child bond is broken. Whenever the child experiences a desire to be with the mother when it cannot, it enters the cognitive state of *separation*. The negative emotional state associated with separation is *anxiety*. Again, the experiencing of separation and anxiety by the child are inevitable. Once the baby is born, it cannot re-enter the womb or return to total dependency. Eventually all mothers learn that without some separation from the child the child's growth is blocked and the mother feels enslaved.

The two types of negative cognitive and emotional states are discerned by mothers by the cries of their child. Much more than fathers, mothers are quickly able to distinguish a cry of frustration from a cry of anxiety. In summary, all children eventually will need to learn to cope with both deprivation and separation. Positive psychospiritual growth depends upon the mother's ability to help her child learn to cope with frustration and anxiety rather than through trying to prevent it totally.

Primary Fear

Every person at one time was a baby and as a baby was totally at the mercy of life forces and people over which there was no control; yet at the same time these others were able to control one's happiness and psychological well-being. This feeling created within each one of us a sense of insecurity. Out of this insecurity every person has the underlying fear of *abandonment*. Abandonment stems from the idea that *I need you to meet my needs and if you go away there will be no one to take care of me anymore. I will be alone and lost and helpless.* This fear of abandonment can continue to affect people even into adulthood if they never have been made to feel special or had their need for security met.

Existential Sin

Out of this fear of abandonment comes the existential sin of the Nurturance Stage—the sin of *egocentrism*. Egocentrism is based on the neurotic fantasy that *self is at the center of one's world*. In this state, a person attempts to control all who are around in order to meet his or her needs. Egocentrism is a defense, and as a defense is neurotic and self-defeating. When one tries to find security in his or her ability to make others do what he or she wants them to do, the person's security is always on shaky ground. As a result the sin of egocentrism, which is found in everyone's life, merely adds to the deprivation and separation we experience. In the process of development we find that the more we try to hold on and cling to others, the more they end up wanting to push us away. This leads to greater emotional states of frustration and anxiety and a greater fear of abandonment. For the child to progress to the next stage of development, he or she will need to take self out of the center of his or her world and put the parents in the middle instead.

NURTURANCE STAGE

Human Responsibility

Primary Responsibility	**Mother**
Major Task	To meet basic physical and psychological needs.
Technique	**Unconditional nurturance**
Focal Point	**Body contact**
Goal	To feel safe within Mother's love.

Psychological Need

Basic Need	**Security**
Resultant Positive Emotion	**Peace**
Psychological State	**Sheltered dependence**
Self-Esteem	I am **special** just because I exist.

Human Fall

	Separation Deprivation
	↓ ↓
Negative Cognitive States	
Resultant Negative Emotions	**Anxiety Frustration**
Primary Fear	**Abandonment**
Existential Sin	**Egocentrism**
Neurotic Fantasy	I am the center of my world.

5
Obedience Stage

Our third psychospiritual stage of development runs from age two to age six and is called the Obedience Stage. The obedience stage of human development corresponds with the Biblical era between the time of Noah and the flood and the giving of the law to Moses on Mount Sinai. During this period the primary focus in the Bible was on faith and obedience. In the same way, the child between ages two and six also needs to learn how to trust and obey. It is during this stage that the issue of authority must be presented and rebellion toward authority must be resolved. The stage begins when the child starts extensively using the word "no." This "no" is a reflection of the child's negative will and egocentrism, which are carried over from the Nurturance Stage. While egocentrism during the Nurturance Stage must be considered normal in the sense that the child does not choose to be egocentric but *is* egocentric, as it continues into the Obedience Stage it becomes a sin. If allowed to continue to develop, egocentrism will eventually create psychological and behavioral problems in the child. Much of what the parents are trying to do in the Obedience Stage is nothing more than trying to help the child gain control of his or her egocentrism so that he or she can eventually move from negative will to positive will. This positive will is necessary after age six for the child to be able to learn and develop skills and competencies.

BIBLICAL BASE

Before we discuss this stage from a theoretical and psychological perspective, we will attempt again to provide a Biblical base for the concepts we will be discussing. Our key passage for this chapter is found in Ephesians 6:1–4:

> Children obey your parents in the Lord; for this is right. Honour thy father and mother; which is the first commandment with promise; that it may be well with thee, and thou may live long on the earth. And ye fathers, provoke not your children to wrath; but bring them up in the discipline and admonitions of the Lord.

There are many other passages that affirm and support this passage in Ephesians. Proverbs 13:24 states, "He that spares the rod hates his son, but he that loves him chastens him diligently." The importance of discipline is also mentioned in Proverbs 19:18: "Chasten thy son while there is hope and let not thy soul spare for his crying." In Proverbs 1:8 the Bible teaches the child to "hear the instruction of thy father and forsake not the law of thy mother." Finally parents are told in Proverbs 22:6 to "train up a child in the way he should go and when he is old he will not depart from it."

The justification for the authority of the parents comes from God and His authority. In this way, authority does not begin with the parents but is delegated to the parents by God. Even more than this, God establishes limits on the use of parental authority and uses Himself as a model. The following Scriptures convey this point. Deuteronomy 8:5 says, "As a man chasteneth his son, so the Lord thy God chastens thee." We also read in Job 5:17, "Happy is the man whom God corrects, despise not the chastening of the Almighty." In Hebrews 12:5,6, we find, "Despise not thou the chastening of the Lord nor faint when thou are rebuked of him: For whom the Lord loveth he chasteneth, and scourgeth every son whom he receiveth." Finally, in Revelation 3:19 it states, "As many as I love I rebuke and chasten." Therefore, the model for parents as they attempt to discipline their children is God, as He attempts to discipline His children. God is our example for the positive use of our authority. These passages also show that the motive behind God's discipline is love. This means that, as parents, our motive when we correct and discipline our children should also be one of love. Being a good Christian parent involves disciplining our children out of a heart of love. Giving a child a spanking without love in our heart provokes the child to wrath and moves that child away from God, not toward Him.

HUMAN RESPONSIBILITY

Any person who thinks that training a child in the way that he should go is an easy process has never been a parent. There are no magical, simple formulas for disciplining children that can be used in all situations. A child is more than a rat that needs to be conditioned; he or she is a living soul created in God's image with a free will. Although parents have been given authority to train and discipline their children, they have not been given a license by God to beat and abuse them. There is a very fine line between spanking a child and abusing a child, which is not determined only by the behaviors of the parent (i.e., the issue of whether spanking should be done by the hand or a stick). Ultimately, child abuse is determined by what is in the heart of the parent. Not all abuse is physical in nature. In fact, many more children are abused psychologically, through such techniques as ridicule and shame, than are abused physically. Either way, as Christians we must vehemently oppose child abuse in whatever form it takes. Because of the strong attack upon spanking today by secular humanists, we must be able to distinguish clearly the difference between correcting a child and beating a child. At the same time, we must continue to affirm the Christian teaching that children are not basically good and that without proper guidance and instruction will not grow up and go the right way. To be good parents, during this stage every parent must acknowledge that, because of the sinful nature within them, they have the potential at any given moment of becoming an abusing parent. This means that we must work hard to allow God's love to control the process of discipline as we allow God to control our lives.

Primary Responsibility

The primary responsibility for establishing authority in the home during the Obedience Stage belongs to the *father*. The Bible clearly indicates that in terms of authority the father is to be the head of the home (Ephesians 5:23). Still, the father must see that his authority was delegated to him by God. This means that for the father to be the seat of authority in the home brings responsibility, not privilege. God holds the father accountable for the use of his authority. He also holds the father accountable for the abuse of his authority and/or the neglect of it.

Most men want to be head of the home; however, most do not understand what this headship really means. Every father will some day stand before God and give an accounting for the way that he disciplined and trained his chilcren. There will be no excuses. If the father abused his authority and hurt his children, he will stand accountable. If the father was too busy and neglected his authority, he will also be held accountable for what happens to his children. No father will be allowed to escape judgment by blaming his wife. The mother will have to account to God for the quality of nurturance she showed to her children, but only the father will give an accounting for the quality of discipline.

There are two major extreme positions that fathers need to stay away from as they attempt to discipline and train their children. The first is authoritarianism. Authoritarianism is defined as the extreme use of authority, primarily displayed in a state of anger rather than love. The authoritarian father tends to lose his temper and, as a result, yells too loud, hits too hard, ridicules too much, and hits too many times. This father usually produces fear in his children when they are young.

If the motive behind our discipline is to be love, it will not produce extreme fear, as seen in I John 4:18. "There is no fear in love, but perfect love casts out fear." The authoritarian father usually finds that the frightened young child turns into a rebellious teenager, defying his authority and going his or her own way.

The other extreme position that a father can take in the use of his authority is permissiveness. Many fathers today spend very little time with their children, especially while they are young. These fathers have largely abdicated their authority and neglected their training and disciplining responsibilities. The excuse most permissive fathers use is that it was the mother's fault the kids did not turn out right. In other words, the permissive father blames the mother when the children do not behave. Instead of disciplining the children as he is supposed to, he yells at the mother instead. Because of lack of control and order in the home (stemming from the vacuum created by the father's lack of authority), the permissive father begins to look for excuses that will allow him to spend more time away from home. Although the mother tries to do her best to keep order in the home, without the father's help she usually fails.

God did not want the mother to be the primary authority figure in the home. This does not mean that she never disciplines the children. Young children below the age of six need to be disciplined immediately after misbehavior, so the mother will have to be involved in the disciplining of the children. Still, the children must not see the mother as the final authority. To the extent that the mother becomes the final authority in the home in the eyes of the children, she loses her capacity to continue as a nurturing mother figure who provides love and a place of refuge. In other words, the mother is never able to be both a mother and a father; but this was never God's plan anyway. God created mothers to be mothers and fathers to be fathers. Although during the Obedience Stage the mother is to have a secondary responsibility for the disciplining and training of her children, her primary role is still to be one of nurturance. The father, then, is to be seen as the seat of authority in the home.

One reason many fathers have sought to escape the responsibility of being the authority figure in the home is because we have created a model that is far too negative. We have tied fathering too much into the role of the bad guy who is always yelling at or spanking his children. No one likes to be the bad guy all the time. This bad guy role was not God's plan for fathers. There is more than spanking children to being a good father and being the seat of power in the home. Disciplining children is only one small part of the father's job. The more important major task of the father is to *foster separation of the children from the mother as he encourages the children to explore their world.* Discipline merely centers around the establishment of safe limits for the children in this process of exploration and discovery. This allows the mother and father to complement each other. He encourages the children to explore, learn, and try things, while she stands ready to comfort them when they get frightened or hurt.

There is a simple principle I try to keep in mind as a father that keeps me from becoming only a bad guy. For every negative, I try to do three positive things with my children. This accomplishes two things. First, if all the reflections of the father to his children are mostly negative, the children begin to think of themselves as bad, which undermines their self-esteem. I want my children to think of themselves as good children created in God's image who sometimes do bad things. When they misbehave or disobey, they need to be punished to remind them not to do these things again. However, each night I still tell them that in spite of the wrong things they sometimes do, they are still special and I love them. Second, I do not want my children to be afraid of me. If I respond with negative feedback every time they are with me, they eventually will not want to be around me. For this reason, I try to do positive things with my children so that they will see me as positive. As we take hikes together, play games together, wrestle on the floor together, and go on trips together, my children come to respect me, not fear me. We must begin to teach more fathers how to be positive dads, not negative ones. The result will be that both the dads and the children will be happier and have more fun.

Major Technique

In the Nurturance Stage the major technique of the mother is one of unconditional nurturance and love for her children. In doing this, she provides a place of safety. For the father the major technique used to establish his authority is *loving discipline with mercy*. In the section where we examined the Scriptural passages associated with this stage, we found that the father was to discipline his children in love in the same way that God disciplines us as His children in love. The focus of this discipline must be upon trying to eliminate wrong behavior. The father must learn to differentiate between attacking the problem behavior and attacking the child. God hates sin but he loves the sinner. As parents, we should dislike those things our children do that they should not, but at the same time we need to love our children always. When we do not distinguish between the behavior and the child, we begin to attack our children and thus undermine their self-esteem. Psychological research clearly shows that as the child's self-esteem goes down, the frequency of emotional and behavioral problems goes up. In other words, if we fathers do not discipline in love, we attack our children's self-esteem, with the result that we get more disobedience and more wrong behavior.

In the same way that fathers are to discipline in love, they also are to discipline with mercy. Too many fathers set up too many rules and try to follow them too rigidly. We are still only dealing with children who are not old enough to go to school. Although a child before the age of six does not understand the idea of intention or motive, a father does. Showing mercy is based on the ability of the father to distinguish willful, wrong behavior from ignorant or unintentional wrong behavior. As an example, my five-year-old son was playing catch with me in the backyard. We were using a real baseball, since that was his desire. In the process of throwing the ball to me, it went crooked and hit and broke a basement window. Now, this action was a wrong behavior, but it was not intentional. It went crooked because he cannot throw very well yet. If there was any fault in this situation, it was mine, for allowing the use of the real baseball before he had the appropriate skills. Showing mercy in this situation involved affirming to him that it was an accident and that he would not be punished. We also decided that it would be best to put away the real baseball until he was older.

Showing mercy is based upon knowing when to uphold a rule and when to make an exception. Never having an exception to a rule is rigid behavior and is asociated with authoritarian fathers. Always finding exceptions to the rule is a sign of weakness and is associated with permissive fathers. The good father is one who can find a middle ground between authority and mercy while showing both in love.

Focal Point

So far this chapter has focused upon the father's primary role in establishing authority in the home during the Obedience Stage. As all children come into the Obedience Stage as egocentric, self-centered individuals who can only focus on their own needs, they must leave the stage with the knowledge that there are other people in this world and no one can always be the center of attention or get everything they want. The person who is responsible for challenging this egocentrism within each child is the father. Because of their sinful nature, the children come into this stage wanting to be the center of their life, and, in this way, be like God. Through loving discipline the father must get the child to take self off the throne and put dad on it. Instead of the child being lord of his or her own life, the father needs to become lord. The focal point of the Obedience Stage, therefore, is that the father needs to *be the boss*.

Children need to learn that their will is not the final authority and to live within limits. The goal for the father in being the boss is not to break the will of those under his authority, but to encircle the will of his children with his strength and with his love. The purpose of this encircling is not to hurt or destroy the children but to protect them. The word *boss* today has come to take on a negative connotation because we have come to associate it with the word bossy. Boss means final authority and the father is to be the boss of the home. However, this does not mean that he is to become bossy. The father must use his physical and spiritual strength to help each of his children gain control of the egocentric will inside them. To lose egocentrism is not bad, but good. As children learn when they are young to live under their father's authority, when they become adults they will know how to live under God's authority. In addition, fathers must remember that there is always still another boss, God, watching them, so they must try to do their job in a way that falls within God's standards and limits.

Goal of Stage

The goal of the Obedience Stage is that through the wise use of his authority *the child will come to trust and respect the father, leading to willing obedience.* The goal of the father is not coerced obedience stemming from the child's fear toward the father, but freely chosen obedience stemming from the child's love for the father. It is not enough for the father to focus only on getting obedience from his children. Many fathers get an obedient child when the child is young, but find themselves with a rebellious child when he or she is older. The father who tries to frighten the child into obedience is actually working to break or destroy the will of the child, not encircle it with his love. True obedience in children comes when they want to obey their parents. It is this desire to please and gain the approval of one's father that will be needed in the next stage.

Children need to do more than just obey their father. They need to look up to and respect him. Willing obedience in a child is always associated with someone whom that child respects. For children to be able to respect their father he must live a life that is worthy of their respect. This includes more than just the way he treats them. It also includes the way he treats their mother and the kind of example he sets for them with his habits and life. Every father should want his children to be able to say proudly to their friends, "That's my dad." To the extent that children respect their father, they will also trust their father. As children trust their dad, they also will come to trust his authority and judgment. In other words, trust and respect cannot be demanded from our children; they must be earned.

As a father fulfills his responsibility to establish authority in the home, his children will be ready to leave home when it is time to go to school. The school systems of this country should be able to expect that the children coming to them already know how to 1) obey authority, and 2) respect authority. To the extent that the child at school is not able to do this, he or she will not be able to learn up to his or her potential. This inability to obey and respect authority directly reflects on the father of that child who has not done his job properly. All children are egocentric and must be taught to obey and respect authority. If a child at school cannot do this, it is the father's fault. The Bible teaches us that mothers are not to blame for disobedient children. The very fact that our school systems today are having a significant problem maintaining order in the classroom and authority in the school shows how far fathers have strayed in living up to their responsibilities as fathers before God. We must see that school systems can only supplement parental authority in a child's life, but never replace it. As Christians, we can see clearly that the problem of discipline in the schools is not the school's fault. The responsibility lies with the parents, and especially the father. Until we can convince fathers to get involved again with their children and establish authority in the home, we will continue to see a breakdown of authority in our schools and in our society.

PSYCHOLOGICAL NEED

Basic Need

In the Nurturance Stage, the basic need of the child was security provided for by a loving mother who was willing to meet the needs of her child. Now, in the Obedience Stage, the basic need of the child is the need for *liberty*. The father has primary responsibility for establishing authority in the home and disciplining his children. The result of his success as a father is that the child begins to gain control of his or her egocentric will and thus obtain freedom. There is a fundamental philosophical conflict today in our society between secular humanism and Biblical Christianity over the true definition of liberty. Secular humanism defines liberty as a social state in which freedom is related to what a person is allowed to do within his or her environment. If the environment and the people in that environment restrict a person's options for choice, that person is not free and does not have liberty. This idea is based upon the humanistic concept of human nature that man is basically good. The humanistic approach is that one can only self-actualize as he or she is freed from the limits of others. The secular humanistic view is that authority and limits are bad because they prevent the person from obtaining liberty. In terms of this period of life between two and six, secular humanists are presently writing and teaching against the use of authority and the use of spanking as a form of discipline. They believe that authority in the home negatively affects the child because it takes away his or her freedom.

The Biblical Christian view is just the opposite. It is based on an acceptance of the sinful nature within each child. The Christian position is that there will not be positive child development without parental intervention and involvement. True freedom is not determined by external social reality, but by an inner spiritual peace. True freedom is not to be found in a place, but in a state of mind. The preschool child who is not disciplined and taught obedience to authority does not become free, but is a slave to his or her own egocentrism. This child is commonly referred to as spoiled. The Biblical view is that true liberty only comes as we learn to live within limits and under authority. It is the disciplined child who has self-control and freedom, not the impulsive one. It is the child who respects and obeys authority who is most able to learn at school. Therefore, secular humanists are right when they say that a child in this stage needs autonomy and freedom. They are wrong, however, when they tell us that liberty can be obtained outside authority and that the child will become responsible all by him- or herself with no parental involvement. A quick look at what has happened over the last twenty years to our society and our schools because of this secular humanistic approach to parenting easily reveals that the Bible is right.

The resultant positive emotion that arises when a child experiences a true sense of liberty is *faith*. As Abraham found that God's authority and guidance was to be trusted, he developed faith in God. It was this faith that allowed him to trust God even when asked to offer his son Isaac as a sacrifice. In this incident God was testing Abraham's heart. As fathers we seek to develop within our children the same simple faith in us that Abraham showed toward God. When a child jumps off a diving board into his father's arms, it is done on the basis of faith that the father will catch him or her. When a child goes to bed at night without fears or nightmares, it is done on the basis of faith that the father will protect him or her. When a child asks his or her father for a gift, it is done in faith that the father will provide for him or her. Children experience true liberty when they have faith in their fathers to take care of them and show them by example the right way to go.

Psychological State

The child's psychological state during the Obedience Stage should be one of *supervisory dependency*. This is different from the sheltered dependency of the Nurturance Stage. In the Nurturance Stage the focus was upon keeping the child from doing things that would be harmful. Here in the Obedience Stage the focus is upon showing the child how to do things. In this stage the child learns how to talk, how to throw a ball, how to jump, how to swing, how to climb, how to ride a tricycle. There are all kinds of things that a child can learn to do. However, most of these things will not be learned very well unless a parent supervises the activity. There are at least two things a child can do without any supervision, and they are watching TV and making a mess. For the child to develop properly in the Obedience Stage, the parents need to see that the child still cannot learn very much or very well without supervision. It is because of this that we say that a child is still primarily dependent and needs the supervision of the parent in order to learn skills.

During the Obedience Stage a child's self-esteem stems from the meeting of the basic need for liberty. Liberty was defined as the state the child experiences as he or she is able to live within the boundaries established by the parents based upon the child's trust in them and their love for him or her. Self-esteem, then, is reflected in the idea that *I am free when I learn to live within limits*. All children need limits for their own safety and protection, as well as their psychological growth and development. Some parents tell their children that they can do anything they set their mind to; however, this statement is just not true. Even without the limits established by the parents, the child still must cope with limits. First, there are the limits of maturation. Every parent of more than one child knows the frustration experienced by a younger child when he or she cannot always do what an older child does. Second, there are the limits of abilities. Not all children have the same abilities. It is hard to be the best in the world in anything. Third, there are the limits of life. Not everyone gets the same opportunities, and not all opportunities come on the basis of objective evaluations of abilities. Children need to learn that life is not always fair. Finally, there are the limits of God. Only God is infinite; man is finite. We live in God's world, not man's, and God places limits on what we can and cannot do. For the child's own well-being and positive self-esteem, he or she needs to learn early in life that there are limits, that all things are not possible, and that one does not always get what he or she desires.

HUMAN FALL

As was already discussed in this section in the Nurturance Stage, because of sin and the fall of man it is impossible for a child to go through the Obedience Stage without being marred psychologically. This is because there is sin in the environment, sin in the parents, and sin in the child. This means that, in the same way that it was impossible for any mother to nurture her child perfectly, it is also impossible for the father to fulfill his responsibilities to discipline and train his children without making mistakes. No father can do a perfect job, but every father is capable of doing a good job. Even when a father disciplines correctly out of love his children still may not initially interpret in the right way what the father did. This idea is found in Hebrews 12:11, where it states, "Now no chastening for the present seems to be joyous, but grievous: nevertheless afterward it yieldeth the peaceable fruit of righteousness unto them which are exercised thereby." This means that even though it is inevitable that children will be marred during this stage because of sin, it is still important that the parents try to do as good a job as they can.

Negative Cognitive States

There are two negative cognitive states that result from improper discipline during the Obedience Stage. The first negative cognitive state is one of *helplessness*. This state of helplessness stems from the use of too much parental authority. The authoritarian parent places too many limits upon the child's behavior and reacts too powerfully when the child does not live within them. This results in the negative emotional state of *fear,* which arises out of the state of helplessness. The child needs to explore and learn, and wants to explore and learn, but does not do so because of fear of the father's wrath. In this way the child is gradually conditioned by the father to remain in a state of total dependency and learned helplessness, and will not try something for fear he or she will make a mistake. This child may begin to withdraw socially and become quiet and shy to stay out of trouble. Too much power used by the parents creates fear in the child and leaves the child in a state of learned helplessness.

The second negative cognitive state associated with the Obedience Stage is *weakness*. Weakness stems from permissive parenting and results when the child has no defined limits or boundaries within which to live. It is the child who is able to live within reasonable limits established by his or her parents who feels strength and confidence. The child who is allowed to throw tantrums, bully other children, steal, and lie feels weak deep down inside. The actions of a spoiled child raised in a permissive home, no matter how violent or aggressive, are the reflection of an inner state of weakness. The bully picks on little kids because he feels weak inside, not because he feels strong. The negative emotional response that results from this state of weakness is one of *anger*. During this time of life this anger is usually controlled by the child's continuing sin of egocentrism, which means that the anger can easily express itself in the form of *rage*. In rage the anger becomes irrational, impulsive, and uncontrollable. When any child begins to react *regularly* from emotional states of rage, the parents need to seek professional help immediately.

In conclusion we are saying here than when children between the ages of two and six have not been taught through loving discipline to live within limits, they will experience a cognitive state of weakness. On the emotional level these children will defend themselves from this state of weakness by attacking their environment in some way as they express their anger.

Primary Fear

The primary fear of all children during the Obedience Stage is that of *punishment*. The preschool child is little and the parents, especially the father, is big. The father's anger can be a scary thing, and the father's discipline can bring pain. No child likes to be punished, and no child likes to experience pain. The pain of the father's spanking is made even scarier by anticipation of it before it happens. Usually the child negatively reacts before the spanking takes place because of this fear of the punishment. Most children eventually try to bargain with the parent in that they promise not to do something again if the parent will not punish them just this one time. Parents should not fall for this strategy of plea bargaining. Although the child's dread is great, the punishment must be meted out in love by the parent. It is only through the continued fear of punishment that the child gradually gains control of his or her egocentric will.

Secular humanists do not believe in punishing children, only in praising them. However, they also do not believe in God or in heaven and hell. What they are seeking is a life with no pain and an eternity with no judgment. If we judge and punish our children, it is only so that they will learn that punishment and pain are a part of life. They are also a part of God's dealing with us as His children. As parents, then, when we punish our children we are only reflecting a larger spiritual reality—that God established standards that we must live up to or He will discipline and punish us. It is not easy to inflict pain upon our children, but as good Christian parents we must if we want them to grow up in the right way.

Existential Sin

The existential sin associated with the Obedience Stage is the sin of *rebellion*. When the child's will is not encircled by the limits of the parent's will, the egocentrism of the Nurturance Stage is allowed to continue. Gradually the child gains more and more power of will as this egocentrism is used to get its own way. By the age of six there are many children who through their tantrums are already in control of the household. If they do not get their way, they scream and yell until they do. If this does not work, they resort to hurting somebody or breaking something until they finally succeed. These children now have more than an egocentric will, they also have a rebellious will. The neurotic fantasy associated with rebellion is the illusion that *I am powerful and parents are weak*. To the extent that children are not disciplined and have not been made to live within limits, they begin to develop a sense of scorn and lack of respect toward their parents. Eventually the permissive parents who spoil their children in the name of love come to be hated by those children for their lack of love, and ridiculed for their lack of conviction. In the end these rebellious children will ignore their parents and do what they want.

On the other hand, children who have been raised in fear by an authoritarian parent also eventually develop a problem with rebellion. However, their rebellion takes more of a passive form than an active one. They rebel through stubbornness, withdrawal, procrastination, and doing things behind their father's back without his awareness.

Sometimes the mother also gets involved in this game of passive rebellion as she supports her children in their attempts to deal with dad's authoritarianism. This father must be helped to see that his authoritarianism is too rigid and that through his rigidity he is driving away from himself the very people that he cares about the most. It is important for this father to seek help so that he can learn to be an authority in the home without becoming authoritarian.

OBEDIENCE STAGE

Human Responsibility

Primary Responsibility	**Father as authority**
Major Task	To promote exploration of the world within safe limits.
Technique	**Loving discipline with mercy**
Focal Point	**Be the boss**
Goal	To trust in father leading to **willing** obedience

Psychological Need

Basic Need	**Liberty**
Resultant Positive Emotion	**Faith**
Psychological State	**Supervisory dependence**
Self-Esteem	I am **free** when I learn to live within limits.

Human Fall

Negative Cognitive States	**Helpless Weak**
Resultant Negative Emotions	**Fear Anger**
Primary Fear	**Punishment**
Existential Sin	**Rebellion**
Neurotic Fantasy	I am powerful and parents are weak and helpless.

6
Behavior Stage

The Behavior Stage covers the period of life between the ages of six and twelve. This stage corresponds with the Biblical Era between the giving of the law to Moses and the time of the Prophets. The emphasis in this stage is upon learning the law in all areas of one's life and, thereby, becoming a law-abiding citizen. Doing right behavior now becomes more important than not doing wrong behavior. Since right behavior must be learned, this stage requires that the child have teachers who instruct him or her in the laws of society and the laws of God. In the Obedience Stage the child needed to learn to obey father as an authority figure out of a somewhat blind trust that the father would take care of him or her. In the Behavior Stage the father must give up some of his authority in the child's life by transferring it to other authority figures who thereby become the child's teachers. The father needs to require that his children show the same obedience and respect for their teachers, in whatever area of learning they are involved, as they did toward him. In this way the father extends his authority out into a broader social context.

Children who have learned to obey their father as an authority during the Obedience Stage will be able to transfer that obedience and respect for authority to their teachers in the Behavior Stage. A willing-ness to listen to teachers as authority figures is the basis for learning right behaviors and developing competencies during the Behavior Stage. The end result of this processs of learning to work hard in order to learn skills is that the child begins to develop a sense of responsibility and self-discipline.

BIBLICAL BASE

The major focus of the Behavior Stage is upon the formal learning of the child, not only in relation to academic learning in the schools, but also in terms of the child learning the laws of society and the laws of God. One of the major problems in our educational system today is that the academic and moral training of our children have been separated from each other. Earlier in the history of our country the school was a place for the teaching of morals and values based on our religious heritage and belief in God. This instruction accompanied the academic training of our children and was considered just as important.

Over the last half of this century our educational system has gradually come under the control of a secular humanistic educational philosophy. This philosophy, derived from an atheistic nonbelief in God, set as its goal within the public school system the separation of the secular from the sacred. This included a separation of academic learning from moral instruction. The purpose of this was to free secular man from traditional moral and religious values capable of controlling society and to create utopia through rational thinking.

To the extent that these educators have been successful, millions of young people growing up today in our society have no sense of purpose or direction to their lives, no sense of social responsibility, and no clear definition of right and wrong. The evidence shows clearly that this trend is negative, as can be demonstrated by the crime, drug addiction, and sexual immorality manifested by these young people who have been programmed with a secular view. What these young people do not have is happiness. We need to return to God's plan, which was that academic learning and moral and religious instruction were to be put together—as can be seen in the following Scriptures.

Our central passage of Scripture, Deuteronomy 6:5-7, best represents what we are discussing in this chapter:

And thou shalt love the Lord thy God with all thine heart, and with all thine soul, and with all thy might. And these words which I command thee this day, shall be in thine heart. And thou shalt teach them diligently unto thy children and shall talk of them when thou sittest in thine house, and when thou walkest by the way, and when thou liest down, and when thou riseth up.

From this passage we learn why there is a spiritual and moral vacuum in our country, and it is not just because the public schools have become more secular. The schools were created to aid parents in their responsibility given by God to educate their children. In this way part of the responsibility for the education of the children was delegated to the public school and the Sunday school. Gradually, though, parents allowed more and more of the instruction to take place at school and at church and did less and less at home. Today millions of parents in our society have gone from delegated authority to abdicated authority, leaving almost all of the education of their children up to the church and school. In the same way that parents have abdicated their authority, they are also now trying to abdicate their responsibility. God will not allow this. Too many parents are blaming the schools for something that God will hold them accountable for—the lack of moral training of their children. Even the Christian school, as an alternative to the decaying public school system, will not be able to make up for lack of moral instruction in the home. We must begin to help parents to pick up once again their responsibility to teach their children diligently about God and about life as commanded by God.

Other passages that affirm the importance of learning can also be found. Proverbs 1:5 tells us that, "a wise man will hear and increase in learning." In this passage we see that wisdom is an important byproduct of appropriate learning. The moral component of learning is seen in Proverbs 9:9,10, where it is stated, "teach a just man and he will increase in learning. For a respect of the Lord is the beginning of wisdom: and the knowledge of the holy is understanding." The value of appropriate learning is also seen in Romans 15:4: "For whatsoever things were written before were written for our learning, that we through patience and comfort of the Scriptures might have hope." In all these Biblical passages it is stressed that learning God's word is of primary importance for all children and adults. Without an understanding of God's word, it is possible to be "ever learning and never able to come to the knowledge of the truth" (II Timothy 3:7) and "professing themselves to be wise they become fools" (Romans 1:22).

From the child's perspective, God instructs children in II Timothy 2:15 to "study to show thyself approved unto God, a workman that does not need to be ashamed, rightly dividing the word of truth."

The value of the Word of God is also affirmed to the child in II Timothy 3:14-17:

> Continue thou in the things which thou has learned and hast been assured of, knowing of whom thou hast learned them. And that from a child thou hast known the holy scriptures which are able to make thee wise unto salvation through faith which is in Jesus Christ. All Scripture is given by inspiration of God and is profitable for doctrine, for reproof, for correction, for instruction in righteousness: that the man of God may be perfect, thoroughly furnished unto all good works.

HUMAN RESPONSIBILITY

During the Behavior Stage there are four important areas in which a child needs to develop a sense of responsibility: home, school, society, and God-church. We will discuss each of these areas briefly.

The *home* is the basic living unit and the place where social responsibility begins and social relationships have their foundation. By the time children reach school age, they need to be given assigned duties in the home. Each child needs to be taught that every member of the family is responsible for the upkeep and cleanliness of the house. Children can learn to make their beds, pick up their belongings and put them away, and help their mother and father around the house. Every child needs to do part of the work but no child should be asked to shoulder more than his or her fair share in relation to other siblings. The work assigned should fit the capabilities of the child and should be evaluated regularly by the parents with constructive feedback. In the home the child also needs to learn the responsibility of how to get along with others. The family needs to work together and take into consideration each other's feelings and needs. Children will not be able to do this unless they are taught. As members of a family, all children need to learn *how to cooperate, how to share,* and *how to give.* In a state of egocentrism, all children know how to be selfish, how to be greedy, and how to be bossy. The roots of overcoming this egocentrism must begin in the home as the parents teach their children how to work together as a family.

A second area in which the child needs to learn responsibility is in *school.* Although all children cannot be expected to be A students, they can apply themselves and work diligently to learn within their potential. Basic academic skills in the areas of reading, writing, and arithmetic are essential to life and the child's future happiness. At the same time, parents must acknowledge that formal learning is not easy.

For children to learn up to their potential, they need good teachers and parents who support the educational system. Parents need to reinforce the efforts of the school to educate their children by also placing a high priority on education. They need to support the teacher, affirm that the children should obey the school authorities, and make sure that they do their homework. Finally, parents should instruct their children to follow the same principles of cooperation, sharing, and giving with friends at school that they learned with brothers and sisters at home. They should also be encouraged to make friends with many children rather than egocentrically becoming involved with only a few.

The third area in which a child needs to learn responsibility is in *society.* If a child receives a bicycle, he or she should be taught how to ride it safely within the laws established by society for operating it on the road. Children should be taught not to litter by instruction and by example. As children are taught specific laws of society, they also need to be taught the importance of the principle of law—that without law there is no social order. Police officers should be respected, not undermined or ridiculed. Within social law each child needs to learn that it is wrong to steal, lie, or cheat. Finally, each child needs to be taught the principle of service to one's community. In all of these areas, the best way for the child to be taught is through the parent's example. Parents themselves need to be law-abiding citizens living with a social conscience concerned about the needs of others and the needs of their community.

The fourth area in which the child needs to learn responsibility is in relation to *God.* This responsibility is learned through the child's involvement in a local church. Through this church involvement, the child should learn about God, Jesus Christ, sin, confession, forgiveness, and love. Beyond their involvement as children in a church, they also need to see the importance of God reflected in the lives of their parents. Therefore, parents should live before their children as examples of God and His love for them. Other important areas are family discussions of spiritual principles, family prayer, and family involvement in reaching out to others. As children experience the reality of God and His love working in their lives through such family activity, they will be drawn closer to God.

Each set of parents must define for themselves the specific behaviors they want to promote and develop within their children in these four areas. God's Word, however, should be their base for establishing which behaviors are most important so they can set priorities. In reality, there is a finite limit as to the abilities of each child and a finite amount of time available for learning. Because no child can be an expert in everything, parents must make choices during this stage as to what skills they want their children to learn as well as how well they want their children to learn that skill. During this stage, however, parents should refrain from tying up all of a child's learning ability in only a few activities.

Primary Responsibility

The primary responsibility for the education of children during the Behavior Stage is given by God to the *parents,* not to the school. Parents are responsible for the kind of education their children get and are accountable for what they learn. This is the basis for community control of our public school system through the establishment of a local school board. As Christians, we need to fight for the continuation of local control of our public schools rather than the centralization of control, either at the state or federal level. The less local control there is of the local school system, the less parents will be able to voice their concerns over the education their children are receiving. It has also become apparent that the secular humanistic philosophy of education can most easily be established at higher levels of authority. Today, a few people at the federal level can implement policies that effect our children over which the local community and parents have no control. This lack of ability to stop the secular changes being made in our public school system has led many Christian parents to withdraw their children from the system and place them in private schools where local control is still possible.

Care must be taken, however, that we do not place too much emphasis on which school our child attends. As already discussed, the academic learning of children is only one of four areas where parents need to be involved in what their children are learning. This means that the parents' responsibility for the proper development of their children during this stage is much more than just a decision as to what school they will attend. Instruction in values and morals must begin in the home and must be given by the parents. *Parents are to be the primary teachers of their children in all areas of the children's life.*

The parents' role as teachers does not end when the child enters school; it really only begins. It is not right and wrong that was learned during the Obedience Stage, but the willingness to obey and the certainty of punishment when the child did not obey. Actual moral education in the positive sense does not begin until the Behavior Stage. For the parents to be successful during this stage, they must gradually shift from the role of boss to the role of teacher, especially the father. This is not because the father is no longer the authority figure in the home. It is merely because punishment as a technique is not a successful strategy for obtaining good behavior.

The secondary responsibility for our children during the Behavior Stage rests on all those who formally and informally become our children's teachers. This may include many different people: the mother of a child your children play with, a babysitter, a Sunday school teacher, a school teacher, a Cub Scout or Brownie Scout leader, a coach of some athletic team, a music teacher, a minister, a police officer, and a lifeguard at the swimming pool. The list is endless. Everywhere your child goes where new skills are taught and developed there is someone who is a teacher of children. The task of educating children belongs on a secondary level to the whole society. The whole society has a stake in the children of today who will become the adults of tomorrow and must see that they are taught constructive rather than destructive morals and values. To the extent that individual children do not learn constructive values, the whole society eventually suffers.

One word of caution needs to be given. Two groups need to be excluded from being the teachers of our children. The first is other children. Although a few children, especially by high school, show the maturity necessary to teach younger children, most teenagers are still too young and egocentric to be allowed to be your children's teachers unless there is proper adult supervision. In our society, too many children are learning from other older children the values and morals that are controlling their lives. Through peer group influence and peer group pressure, many children are being led into alcoholism, drug addiction, sexual immorality, and rebellion against parents. This decay would not have been possible if there had not already existed a vacuum in our children because of a failure by parents and teachers to teach right moral values.

The second segment of our society that should not have the freedom to teach our children are those adults who believe in and teach values contrary to and destructive to the basic political and religious freedoms upon which this nation was founded. Criminals should not be allowed to teach our children openly how to lie, cheat, and steal. People who are immoral should not be allowed to teach our children openly immorality. Political revolutionaries should not be allowed to teach our children openly how to commit acts of violence that ultimately undermine our nation's governmental system. Finally, people who do not believe in God should not be allowed to teach our children openly to take the name of God in vain. All of these things are self-destructive to us as a society and will eventually lead to social deterioration and a loss of personal freedom.

Major Task

The major task of parents as teachers, as well as other adults as teachers of our children, is to *help our children develop character*. Today this word *character* is for many people an old-fashioned or outdated concept. To live one's life by principles that extend beyond one's own egocentric desires is becoming a scarce commodity. Character develops from the premise that, in terms of society and in terms of God, not all values are equal. Character is based upon the child being taught the difference between values that are transitory and values that are permanent, values that bring short-term pleasure and values that bring long-term happiness, and values that destroy relationships and values that build relationships.

Once again our conflict as Christians over values clarification is with secular humanism. Secular humanism as a philosophy has no source of authority beyond man and, therefore, has no absolute values. All values under this system become relative and, thereby, equal. As all values become equal, there is no longer any base for concepts of right and wrong. Right and wrong now merely become the reflections of what each individual desires to do, which leads us back to the sin of egocentrism. Values clarification in our public school system in the hands of secular humanistic educators is no longer values clarification at all. The goal of this movement is not to clarify values, but to destroy them.

The same is true of the situation ethics movement in theology. The stated goal of this movement is to free us from the letter of God's law by moving us to a higher plane called "the spirit of God's law." After twenty years of situation ethics in our Christian colleges, seminaries, and churches, all it has accomplished in the name of Christian theology is the destruction of basic Christian values. Some of the most intolerant, rigid, dogmatic, and vindictive people in our society are the very same liberal Christians who are preaching a gospel of love while condoning lives of sin.

In order for parents to teach values, they must have values; in order for children to learn character, they must be taught character by parents who have character. The problem we find ourselves with today is an adult generation moving away from God, living by values of self-consumption, personal pleasure, and materialistic greed. It is no wonder that the children of today are confused. Children are being taught values by their parents that they can see clearly do not bring happiness. On the one hand, they can see the emptiness of these values in their own parents' lives, yet they still try to live by them because they are not aware of other alternatives. If we live with only a relative set of values established on the human level, we are lost on the sea of life, ready to be drowned by the raging waters. It is time that we rediscover that there is only one source of values that are eternal—those that come from God. The beginning of building character in our children starts as we teach them the Word of God, and as we as parents build our lives and our values around its teachings.

Technique

Character, if it is to be developed, is not something that can be built overnight. The building of character in our children takes effort and time. There are no shortcuts to the development of character, and we cannot buy it for our children with money. The technique needed is *diligent instruction with patience*. The term *diligent* is defined here as "fulfilling one's responsibility with care and determination." The focus is on being concerned with details. When God asks us to be diligent in the teaching of our children, He wants us to do it with great attention to details and with a desire that it be done right. The term *patience* implies that the teaching and training of our children will take time. The process of learning requires that a task be repeated over and over again until it is mastered. Sometimes, it is easy for the teacher who finds a skill or task to be simple to forget all the hard work and effort it took in order to reach that level of proficiency. Every new skill a child learns must be acquired through hard work, effort, and practice. A good teacher is one who can continue to instruct a child patiently without becoming overly frustrated because learning does not take place immediately.

In this process of instruction a good teacher is one who also learns the importance of praise. Where in the Obedience Stage the primary focus was upon the father as an authority figure punishing wrong behavior, in the Behavior Stage the focus must be on parents as teachers praising right behavior. Many parents who are successful during the Nurturance and Obedience Stage fall apart completely during the Behavior Stage. One problem for these parents is that they do not know what are appropriate and inappropriate uses of authority. After the age of six, the use of spanking as a means of affirming who is the boss should only be used when the issue is one of direct defiance of parental authority. The inability of a seven-year-old son to throw the ball the way his father wants him to is not an example of defiance of authority, but lack of skill development. Instead of spanking him or yelling at him for doing it wrong, the father needs to praise his son when he does it right, while continuing to instruct him patiently when he does it wrong. In this case the father wrongly tries to demand obedience in an area where the son does not have the capacity to obey. In reacting this way the father is placing unrealistic expectations on his son which work to undermine self-esteem.

You cannot get right behavior in terms of skill development over a period of time by punishing a child. You get right behavior through *praise and practice*. Even in the area of moral development a parent should not expect immediate success. It takes time for a child to initiate moral judgments on his or her own. The problem for many parents is that they do not praise their children enough. The secret of being a good teacher is an effective use of praise.

It is also important that parents as teachers *focus must of their praise on the child's effort rather than on the child's performance*. There are many parents who praise their children a lot but are still ineffective because they focus on the wrong thing. If all the praise is reserved for the child's performance, self-esteem is directly tied only to performance. Because children during skill development almost always make some mistakes during performance, they either do not receive praise or the praise they do receive becomes flattery. Since, in reality, there is no objective standard against which the child is competing, connecting the praise of the child to performance creates significant amounts of anxiety and pressure and in the long run undermines self-esteem through demands for perfection. As Christian parents and teachers, we must praise our children according to the same standard by which God evaluates. God is not concerned that we always win, but only that we do our best. As parents, we should *praise our children for doing their best.* In this way they can all become winners.

Another problem in relation to praise relates to the values in our society. Much of what we praise in our children is not a result of effort but of unearned attributes and abilities given by God. The three most obvious attributes that we overly value in children are female beauty, athletic abilities, and intelligence. Many parents, for example, praise their children only for the grades they get. Too much importance is thereby given to the grades. As an example, parents might praise a lazy child who, because of his inborn intelligence, get A's in school, but criticize a second child who works hard but who, because of his intellectual potential, gets C's. Both children now have the potential for problems—one develops a low self-esteem because of false guilt, while the other develops an artificially high self-esteem leading to false pride. What we must learn to do if we want to be successful teachers is to *evaluate and give feedback to children on the basis of their own potential.* In the end, character is built as children learn to compete with themselves in order to be the best that they can be, not as they compete with other children to win grades, medals, and beauty contests.

Focal Point

The focal point for the Behavior Stage is that parents and other adults have a responsibility to *teach values and skills.* On the one hand, children need to develop abilities and talents to the extent that they can have a sense of mastery. On the other, children need to understand that self-esteem is not built on skills and talents alone, but on how those skills and talents are used. In the beginning the child, out of his or her egocentric orientation, develops abilities to draw attention to self. Parents and teachers must begin to show children that the higher value of the skills they learn is ultimately in how those skills can be used to serve others and serve God. The teaching of skills and values must go hand in hand if we are to build true character in our childen and move them beyond egocentric self-centeredness. To separate the teaching of academic learning from moral principles is to undermine our child's psychological well-being as well as his or her sense of social responsibility. For these reasons we, as Christians, must be in favor of values clarification in the home, in the school, and in the church. If parents do not like the values being taught their children, they should have the freedom to try and change the system or withdraw from it.

Goal of Stage

The goal of the Behavior Stage is that *through positive encouragement by teachers the child learns perseverance and self-discipline.* Many of the skills the child is going to learn during childhood are only short-term. More important than what activity a particular child gets involved in is that they get involved. In this involvement all children will find themselves in a conflict between the desire they have to learn a skill and the pain and sacrifice necessary to fulfill this desire. The principle of egocentrism leads to a prediction that most children will want to quit when they find they cannot immediately do something. The child wants to ride a bicycle *now,* just as he wanted a cookie "now" when he was younger. The problem is that parents cannot give their children skills on demand or buy them with money. Parents can buy their child a piano, but they cannot buy or give their child the immediate ability to play it. Playing the piano and learning to ride a bicycle both take time. To master either skill requires perseverance and self-discipline. Too many parents are allowing their children to quit an activity during this stage of life because it is "too hard." Every new activity is hard, and good parents make their children stay with it until it is successfully mastered. The principle of mastering skills, once it is started, therefore, is more important than the specific skills mastered during the Behavior Stage.

PSYCHOLOGICAL NEED

Basic Need

In terms of our hierarchy of basic human needs, the need associated with the Behavior Stage is *competence*. Competence is based on a child's ability to learn and master skills and information. Every child has a need for competency. The real issue concerns the true meaning of competency. The question that needs to be raised concerns who the child is competing with for this need. If the child is always made to compete with other children or evaluated only in relation to other children, competency will depend on whether this child is better than the others. Although this may not have been our intention, the high value that our society places on winning or being the best has undermined the sense of competency in most children. Most attributes and talents distribute themselves on the basis of the normal bell-shaped curve, where most children are average and only a few are gifted. If we associate competency with giftedness in any particular skill, a few children will be able to think of themselves as successes, while most will think of themselves as failures. Any child who thinks of him- or herself as a failure will no longer have a sense of competency. Younger children in a family may always come up short when they are compared with older siblings. This also destroys the child's sense of competency.

When the child's sense of competency is undermined in this way, the child will gradually begin to try less. This is exactly the opposite of what many parents intend. The hope of these parents is that by comparing the child with others who are more successful the child will become motivated to try harder. This just will not happen. Instead, what we need to do is determine competency on the basis of the effort the child gives in relation to his or her own potential. For competency to be obtained, the child must be taught to compete with him- or herself, rather than always trying to compete with others. In competition with others only a few can win, but in competition with self all can win and all can meet their need for competency.

It is absolutely essential that all children during this psychospiritual stage find something at which they can be successful.

The need for competency assumes that every child has the ability to learn skills, and the more skills the child learns the greater his or her sense of competency. Children on their own will naturally compare themselves with others, so it is wise for parents to find some special area in which each of their children can have a unique sense of competency. This is especially true among siblings. Each child within the family should be encouraged and helped to find a special activity or ability that he or she can do better than anyone else in the family. This will give the child a special sense of value and will prevent the sibling rivalry and jealousy that can take place if all the children in the family only learn the same skills.

The resultant positive emotion that stems from a sense of competency over the ability to do something well and through the true mastery of a skill is *humility*. Humility does not come about when a child competes with others and wins. This only creates false pride. True humility develops when a person competes with and overcomes his or her own limitations. As one is able through hard work and effort to accomplish something or reach a goal, there is a quiet self-confidence that follows, creating in the person the feeling of humility. Out of humility a child no longer sees other children as enemies to conquer but as friends to encourage. In this way a child can be pleased not only with his or her own achievements, but can also be happy for the achievements of peers.

Psychological State

The psychological state during the Behavior Stage is one of *dependence/independence*. The word *dependence* is given first because the child is still more dependent than independent. Parents must meet the child's basic needs and make choices and decisions for the child. In terms of learning, parents must make the final decision as to what activities the child will attempt to master and must oversee the practice time involved. Parents are also responsible for encouraging and praising the child so that the child will not become discouraged. Finally, it is up to the parents to keep the child going in the early stages of skill mastery and not allow the child to quit until the skill is learned.

On the other hand, the child also is becoming increasingly independent. Although parents can provide learning opportunities for their children, motivation for learning must come from the child. During this stage the child begins to make decisions and assert his or her will in the family. The process of going to school also creates independence in the child. Significant amounts of time now must be spent away from the parents and their authority. Children are required to choose whether they will follow through with the principles they have been taught at home when they are at school, playing with friends, or staying overnight at a friend's house. During this stage parents need to begin to teach their children responsibility by giving each child responsibility. However, to give a child responsibility also means that parents must give the child the freedom to fulfill that responsibility on his or her own.

Self-Esteem

During the Behavior Stage self-esteem is tied up with the fulfillment of the need for competency. To build self-esteem in their children during this stage, parents need to set up opportunities for their children to learn and master skills. In the learning process a child needs to be praised rather than criticized, with the focus more on the child's effort than on his or her performance. At the same time, parents need to acknowledge the developing autonomy and maturity in their children by giving them responsibilities and the freedom needed to fulfill them. Self-esteem develops when a child is successful in what he or she is doing. Success gives the confidence to try other, harder activities. The root of self-esteem should be based on the philosophy stated simply as *I am a success when I do my best*. This means that positive self-esteem stems from helping each child reach his or her own potential rather than only beat other children in competition.

HUMAN FALL

No matter how well parents follow these guidelines, there will still be problems. Because we live in a society in which competition affects us all, no child will be able to ignore a comparison with others completely. As a result, all children in this stage, as in the ones before, will be psychologically marred. Sin is still the ever-present reality in each child's life, stemming from the environment, from parents, from teachers, from peers, and from self. During this stage all children will experience at least one situation in which someone hurts them by making fun of them or they do not reach a goal that they set, which disappoints them. As a result each child must learn to cope with these hurts and disappointments.

Negative Cognitive States

There are two negative cognitive states that can arise in the Behavior Stage. The first is the state of *superiority*. The feeling of superiority occurs in children who have been praised extensively for abilities or attributes that they did not earn. In most cases, these children place too much of their self-esteem in a few areas because they get so much attention and recognition from them. Much of the blame for this can be placed on the parents. Children who begin to act superior do so because their parents are pushing them. Many times their parents are using the child's abilities and talents to deal with their own feelings of inadequacy and low self-esteem. The negative emotion that accompanies the state of superiority is *conceit*. Some examples of areas in which children can develop this problem are the wealth of parents, the social status of parents, the I.Q. of the child, the athletic abilities of the child, the child's physique or beauty, and an opportunity the child might get to be the lead in a church musical or school play. The underlying principle behind superiority is that a person puts him- or herself up by putting others down. In reality, the reason for this child's feelings of conceit is not due to too much self-esteem or self-love, but because he or she has too little. Children who operate from a state of superiority do so not because they feel strong, but because they feel weak and vulnerable. As an example, a bright child who finds all of the attention of his parents focused only on what grades he gets eventually begins to feel extreme amounts of anxiety and pressure over grades and tests. The problem is that this child has no other outlet for self-esteem, so that if he should ever do poorly in school his self-esteem would be destroyed.

The point here is that whenever self-esteem is tied to performance, even in a child who always seems to win, the child is always only one mistake away from being a failure.

The second negative cognitive state associated with the Behavior Stage, is that of *failure*. For the child who succeeds, the problem becomes one of the fear of failure. However, based on secular values, most of the children in our society today think of themselves as failures. In the world of competition success is only reserved for a few, while failure is the fate of most. Thirty kids in a fifth-grade class enter a spelling contest—one wins and twenty-nine lose. By the world's judgment all twenty-nine failed in the task of winning the contest. We make superstars out of winners and pay them a lot of money. We cast the average person into a life cursed by its mediocrity and lack of "importance." We call A students winners and all the rest losers.

Failure has come to be determined by a standard outside the reach of most children. In other words, they are failures because they were born that way. They were failures before they ever started to learn. The state of failure arises from a philosophy that winning is more important than trying and doing your best. The negative emotion associated with the state of failure is one of *shame*. Shame is an important emotion when children experience it at a time that they have truly disappointed someone or not lived up to their potential because it causes them to try harder next time. On the other hand, some children are made to feel ashamed merely because they did not learn or accomplish something that was beyond their potential. This is false shame, and it undermines the child's self-esteem, creating psychological problems. The usual reaction of these children who feel like failures is that they stop trying because they become afraid of the risk involved.

Primary Fear

Both groups of children, those in a state of superiority and those in a state of failure, fear *disapproval*. The primary orientation of children during the Behavior Stage, who have learned to obey and trust authority, is the desire to please and gain the approval of parents and teachers. On this basis all children want to be judged competent by their parents and teachers so that they can receive praise. The child in a state of superiority receives flattery rather than praise, while the child in a state of failure receives criticism and punishment rather than praise. In the end both types of children fear the disapproval of their parents. Those in a state of superiority attempt to escape disapproval by trying to be perfectly perfect. Those in a state of failure attempt to escape disapproval by trying to become perfectly worthless. Both efforts are actually hidden attempts at expressing hostility toward parents who have undermined the self-esteem of the child through too much pressure and too many unrealistic expectations.

Existential Sin

The existential sin that both groups of children—those which are trying to be perfectly perfect and those which are trying to be perfectly

---

BEHAVIOR STAGE

Human Responsibility

Primary Responsibility	**Parents as teachers**
Major Task	To help children develop character.
Technique	**Diligent instruction with patience**
Focal Point	**Teach values and skills**
Goal	Through positive encouragement by teachers to learn perseverance and self discipline.

Psychological Need

Basic Need	**Competence**
Resultant Positive Emotion	**Humility**
Psychological State	**Dependence/Independence**
Self-Esteem	I am a **success** when I do my best

Human Fall

	Failure Superiority
Negative Cognitive States	↓ ↓
Resultant Negative Emotions	**Shame Conceit**
Primary Fear	**Disapproval**
Existential Sin	**Pride**
Neurotic Fantasy	I may not be perfect, but you are less perfect than I.

---

worthless—have is the sin of *pride*. The problem of pride in both cases
is associated with the desire for perfection. As Christians, we understand that those people with a desire for superiority have a problem
with pride, but we have not adequately understood how those who talk
about how much of a failure they are and how worthless they are also
have a problem with pride. In many Christian circles we have actually
come to label this latter type of person as one having humility. In this
case, humility is defined as the ability to put yourself down and be a
failure. True humility has already been defined as the positive emotional state that accompanies the fulfillment of our need for competency as we learn to do our best. Pride has its roots, then, in both an
overvaluation and undervaluation of our potential as created by God. In
both cases the people feel unfairly judged by others, and the sin of
pride is the rejection of that judgment. The neurotic fantasy associated
with pride centers on the idea that *I may not be perfect, but you are less
perfect than I.* In other words, people with a problem in the area of pride
constantly find ways to defend themselves against the possibility of disapproval by finding flaws in others and attacking before they can be
attacked. Children in a state of failure direct their attack toward parents and authority figures, while those in a state of superiority direct
their attack against their peers.

7
Motive Stage

The Motive Stage runs from age twelve to age twenty and is associated with the Biblical Era from the time of the Prophets up to the sending of God's Son, Jesus Christ. The message of the Prophets always centered on the word *repent*. The people were instructed over and over that they needed to repent and turn from their wicked ways. This was the message of John the Baptist, the last prophet: "Repent ye: for the kingdom of heaven is at hand" (Matthew 3:2). God's message of repentance in the Motive Stage is a natural response to the problem of the sin of pride, which developed in the Behavior Stage. In the Biblical Era after the time of Moses the focus was on the use of the sacrificial system to atone for sin because of man's inability to live up to the law. The Jews, however, were a proud people and eventually changed the law through interpretations of it to such an extent that, by the time of the Prophets, they felt they were capable of following the law and, thereby, through human effort had earned their place as God's people.

In the same way, children during the Behavior Stage come to feel that right behavior, good performance, and being a success are all that is needed to become a mature adult and find happiness. Even many adults still find themselves trapped in trying to find satisfaction and happiness through behavior, through their doing. But just as works are not enough to obtain eternal life, neither is work enough to bring happiness to life. In the Motive Stage the child must go beyond performance to the problem of relationship in order to gain the acceptance of others, including peers. For this task teenagers must struggle with the issue of what they are as a person on the inside, not just what they show on the outside. The issue of *becoming* is more important to continued psychospiritual development than the issue of *doing*. This does not mean that doing stops. It only means that the child must begin to understand the why questions behind their behavior. Important why questions for the adolescent are: 1) Why do I lose my temper so much?; 2) Why do I feel jealous when my friend has a date?; 3) Why do I feel so lonely?; 4) Why do I fight with my parents?; 5) Why do I always feel as if nobody likes me?; 6) Why am I afraid to say what I think?; and 7) Why do I feel uneasy when people look at me? All of these questions relate to the issue of self-acceptance and require that the teenager develop insight into the meaning of feelings and motives.

BIBLICAL BASE

In Exodus 3:15 God referred to Himself through the phrase "I AM THAT I AM." This clearly indicates that God does not have a problem in terms of self-acceptance and self-actualization. God is not in the process of becoming, like man, but is already totally self-actualized. Since God has no identity crisis, God does not need man to fulfill His identity.

However, the problem that teenagers have during the Motive Stage arises from a sense of alienation and strangeness created by their search for human identity. Secular psychology teaches that this sense of alienation, or what is commonly called the "identity crisis," is brought about by a lack of integration of self. In other words, the self is fragmented into parts and cannot seem to be put back together by the teen, creating in him or her a state of confusion. As Christians, we must reject this idea that the primary alienation of adolescence is that of self from self, or even self from parents, since the origin of this problem is the alienation of man from God. This means that teenagers today are seeking through the peer group a social solution—acceptance of self by others—to what is primarily a spiritual problem—acceptance of self by God. On the other hand, humanistic psychologists are trying to offer only a psychological solution—acceptance of self by self—and many Christians have also wrongly fallen for this approach.

For the first time the teenager in the Motive Stage begins to realize that human nature always exists in a state of conflict. This truth is reflected by Paul in Romans.

> For that which I am doing I do not understand; for I am not practicing what I would like to do, but I am doing the very thing that I hate. For I know that nothing good dwells in me, that is, in my flesh; for the wishing is present in me, but the doing of the good is not. For the good that I wish, I do not do, but I practice the very evil that I do not wish. I find then the principle that evil is present in me, the one who wishes to do good. Wretched man that I am! Who will set me free from this body of death.
>
> *Romans 7:15–24*
> *(New American Standard Version)*

This passage points out the reality that all children run into during adolescence—the destructive power of their own egocentrism. Teenagers want to love their parents, but continually find themselves in a state of anger and rebellion toward them. In terms of close friendships, teenagers want to be liked but continue to do things that bring rejection. The most frustrating aspect of the Motive Stage is that the egocentric self always seems to win, destroying relationships and bringing unhappiness and loneliness.

To understand why adolescents have this problem, we must come to understand the part of the human personality which in the Bible is labeled the heart. Within this heart there is a sinful nature, a flesh, that all human beings have. This sinful nature came as a result of the fall of man and its control continues in our lives as long as we remain in the state of separation from God. This truth is presented in Jeremiah 17:9,10, where it is stated, "The heart is deceitful above all things and desperately wicked: who can know it? I the Lord search the heart, I try the reins, even to give every man according to his ways, and according to the fruit of his doings." The teen tries to cope with this problem of sin first by trying to fool him- or herself: "Every way of man is right in his own eyes: but the Lord ponders the heart" (Proverbs 21:2). As a second defense he or she also tries to fool others: "You are they which justify yourselves before men; but God knows your hearts" (Luke 16:15). In the end, though, the problem of acceptance does not go away because no one can ever fool God.

The Bible teaches that all are accountable to Him and will be judged by Him. Up to this point the judgments on the child came from others mostly in the form of how well he or she performed right behaviors. The teenager eventually must learn that acceptance by others, by self, and by God is not determined by works, but by the inner motives of the heart. We see the difference between man's perception and God's perception in I Samuel 16:7: "For the Lord sees not as man sees; for man looks on the outward appearance; but the Lord looks on the heart." At I Chronicles 28:9, we see that God evaluates us on the basis of inner motives: "For the Lord searches all hearts and understands all the imaginations of the thoughts." This is also affirmed at I Kings 8:39, where it states, "even thou only know the hearts of all the children of men." Finally, in Psalm 44:21 we read, "shall not God search this out? for he knows the secrets of the heart." Therefore, in the Motive Stage, it is not enough that we gain the acceptance of others, we must all eventually gain the acceptance of God. This is done through a belief in the substitutionary atonement of Jesus Christ, who through his death on the cross, paid the penalty for our sin. We can begin to become free from our bondage to self only as we deal with our separation from God. This freedom starts with a belief in Jesus Christ as our Savior.

HUMAN RESPONSIBILITY

Two areas on which the adolescent needs to focus during the Motive Stage are the task of learning to *identify feelings* and the child's ability to *understand his or her motives*. In terms of feelings, it is not so much that the child has never expressed feelings before, since feelings have been expressed since birth, but that the child now begins to recognize the effects these feelings have on others. The negative feelings, such as jealousy, envy, hatred, and lust, present the greatest problems. Also, for the first time in life the child finds him- or herself capable of experiencing mood states that endure for a long period of time. The anger of the earlier stages may have been more intense, but it was usually gone quickly. In adolescence the emotional moods, especially the mood of loneliness, may last for days. Because teenagers do not understand where these moods come from or how they operate, they tend not to want to talk about them. Many times teens are not even aware of the mood states they are in until they have been in them for several hours or days. One of the main tasks of the Motive Stage is that teens learn to identify their feelings and moods so that they can better control the affect they can have on self and on interpersonal relationships.

The second area all teenagers need to deal with is one of understanding human motivation. Human relationship is a very complicated process in which two people can perform the same behavior for totally different reasons. The teenage girl needs to discover that there are other reasons why a boy might say the words "I love you" than on the basis of real love. The inability to understand the motives of others opens teenagers to manipulation and hurt. The inability of teens to understand their own motives also opens them to misunderstanding and attack. The ability to understand our own motives as well as the motives of others provides the foundation upon which we can eventually build intimacy and friendship. If teenagers have not yet learned to understand their inner motives, the relationships that develop will remain only on a superficial level. In this process of inner discovery teens must refrain from blaming all personal suffering on the failure of others. What we find is that most teens find it easier to find flaws in other people, especially their parents, than to find flaws in themselves.

From a Christian perspective, adolescents need to understand the spiritual implications of their feelings and motives. The first step is to learn that other people do not cause our negative feelings, our own inner wrong motives do. The usual approach to dealing with negative feelings is to blame them on others and then to try to make others change so that we can feel better. The Christian view is that our negative feelings stem from evil motives in our heart and, as a result, are caused by our own sin. This means that we will not be able to deal successfully with negative emotions until we can change ourselves.

A second problem that confronts teens is their inability to distinguish love from lust in their dating relationships. Too many teens are calling lust love and using it as a basis for building a long-term dating or marriage relationship. As we can easily see today, this is just not working. The Bible teaches us that lust is a sin that stems from wrong motives in the heart and we are warned against using it as a basis for marriage and love. Since much of the turmoil experienced during adolescence centers around the process of dating, it is important that we be able to help our young people understand that there is a difference between physical attraction and love.

As Christian parents, we must teach our teenagers that sin begins as motives in the heart, not in our behaviors or in feelings that we have. The outward acts of sin are merely reflections of an inward attitude of sin. Too often in the church today we focus only on righteous living—doing right behaviors and not doing wrong behaviors—when what we need to do is focus more on a right heart. To focus only on the behaviors of sin is to whitewash the outside while leaving the inside dirty. This only makes people like the Pharisees, pious and self-righteous, with a problem of pride.

Teens need more than changed behavior or catharted feelings if they are to obtain the happiness they seek—they need a changed heart. The real enemy is not a bad environment, bad friends, or bad parents, but a corrupt self.

Primary Responsibility

The primary responsibility for the continued psychospiritual development of a child during the Motive Stage rests on *adults* as models. The direct control of the parents on the child begins to diminish during adolescence, as the child spends more and more time away from the family. Teenagers widen their circle of friends, get involved more fully in extracurricular activities, and assume new responsibilities outside the home. Parents must encourage this venturing out on the part of their children since trying to prevent it would only create psychological problems in the children and emotional turmoil in the home. As models, parents have already largely completed their work during the first twelve years of life—that is, as teens step out more into the world they will begin to reflect what their parents have been to them and taught them. The problem for many parents is that they do not like what they see reflected in their children when their teenagers are given the freedom to begin to make their own choices. If this is true, in most cases the parents usually have failed in some way in dealing with the needs and tasks of the earlier stages. Parents who do not like what they see in their adolescents usually respond by either trying to resume control of their children's lives or by casting them off prematurely. Either approach is wrong and ineffective. The only strategy that will work in this situation is for the parents to stop trying to control or change their children and to start working on changing themselves according to the standards established by God in the Bible. What we find in counseling is that most teenagers are able to change and deal with the conflicts that arise with parents during adolescence when parents are willing to change first.

Still, parents must eventually begin to let go of their children. The best way to do this is through the use of other adult figures as models for their children. Adults who work with teenagers have a responsibility that extends beyond doing their job. They must understand that the teens with whom they are working look up to them and seek to use them as examples of what they want to become in life. If the peer group during adolescence has gained greater control over our children's lives, it is only because our children are finding fewer adults with whom they can identify and can look up to.

Many of the people who have become our children's models are leading lifestyles and reflecting values that are more temporal than eternal. The power of rock music stars and movie stars has become great in its hold on our children, leading them down the road to destruction through drugs, alcohol, and sexual immorality. The question that we might ask concerns why our children are so easily deceived and led astray by these models of hedonism. The answer lies in the failure of parents during the Behavior Stage to teach their children values, as well as skills. The answer also lies in the failure of teachers, coaches, youth directors in our churches, and community leaders to reflect right values in their lives to these teens. The hedonistic lifestyle being lived by young people today is merely a reaction to the materialistic lifestyle of their parents. What is missing in both the parents and their children is love. Where are the adults who want to work with teenagers as models who are willing to give teens what they really need—love? To the extent that those adults who are the models and examples of our young people have become too concerned about themselves and their own needs, they have failed to love the young people with whom they are working. As a result, we as a society are in danger of losing a whole generation of young people, not because of rock music and drugs, but because of our failure to make them feel significant and loved.

The secondary responsibility during this stage is that of peers as friends. Peers are not to be our children's models, but they play an important part in the development of all teenagers. God created man as a social creature with a need for social relationships. An important part of the process of self-discovery comes from the feedback of and interaction with others. The importance of peer friendships during this stage is that they are, as a whole, less threatening. It is with peers that teens can open up and share their thoughts and feelings. This means that we have missed the point in terms of teenage relationships. The purpose of teenage relationships, even for those between teenagers of the opposite sex, should be that of fun and socialization, not dating and sex. As the teenage peer group has moved from its role of building friendships to the role of teaching values, it has become destructive. Values and morals should be taught by parents and adult models, not by peers. When peers gain control of the process of teaching values, egocentrism and hedonism set in, controlled by the conformity and pressure of the peer group which very few adolescents can resist.

Major Task

The major task associated with the Motive Stage is to *help teenagers feel like they are becoming "grownup."* A secondary task is for the parents and adult models to help teens accept as normal their psychological feelings and the physical body changes that take place during this stage. Most adolescents have at least some problems coping with the physical and psychological changes of puberty. As their bodies begin to grow and fill out into adult proportions, teens begin to look in the mirror and wonder whether or not they are okay. This insecurity of self gives power to the peer group. No child wants to look different, act different, or feel different. To be different to the teen is to be abnormal—it means that something is wrong with him or her. As a result, many children try to hide their individuality during this stage, since being too individualistic can bring ridicule and scorn from peers. What the teen is trying to do is merge his or her identity with that of the group and become an extension of the group. Parents and adult models must continue to encourage children to be themselves and reinforce the value of their uniqueness. Somehow these adults must convince the children that psychopathology arises from trying to become something that one is not rather than from being what one is.

A second area in which parents can make their children feel more grownup is in terms of encouraging them to take on more responsibilities and then giving them positive feedback as they prove themselves responsible. In dealing with adolescents, too many parents focus on a child's failures. This makes the teen feel like a little kid and drives him or her toward the peer group. Instead, parents need to keep telling their children how proud they are of them and praise them for their efforts. As the teenager is treated more as a grownup by parents and other adult models, he or she will begin to feel more grownup. The more grownup teenagers feel, the less they will need the peer group, especially in its destructive forms. As teenagers take on more responsibility, parents need to give them more freedom. In the same way that children needed to learn to trust their parents during the Obedience

Stage, parents now need to learn to trust their children in the Motive Stage. The more parents reflect trust to their children, the more their children will act responsibly. On the other hand, the more parents reflect mistrust, the more their children will react irresponsibly.

Technique

The major technique that is to be used during the Motive Stage by parents and adult models is *open communication as equals*. It is recognized that this is sometimes difficult for parents, since at times they may have to revert to their earlier roles of teacher and authority figure. During adolescence children do not want their parents to become their buddies, but still want them to be parents. This means that teenagers can accept that sometimes their parents still will need to instruct them and sometimes still will need to discipline them. The problem for parents is one of discernment and appropriateness. Parents must be able to distinguish the true need of their child in relation to specific problems. Trying to decide whether the child needs discipline, instruction, or communication is the hardest part of being the parent of a teenager, especially when in most cases teens themselves do not know which they need. Regardless, every teenager needs at least some time set aside during which he or she is able to sit down and communicate with his or her parents and be treated as an equal. In the same way, teens seek out adult models who will also treat them as equals. One exception to this is the adult who tries to act like a teenager. Those adults who act like teens eventually are rejected as models. Instead, teenagers want to be treated as adults by adults.

Focal Point

The focal point of how parents and other adults are to make the child feel that he or she is becoming a normal grownup can be summed up in two words—*TALK WITH*. The words *talk with* must be seen in contrast to what the teenager does not need, which is to be "talked at" or "talked about". The focus then must be on dialogue with our children and not a monologue at our children. Too many parents carry on long monologues with their children as they make point after point after point. At the end the parent asks the child if she understands and the child out of self-defense says yes, knowing that if she says no she will get another long monologue. In the same way, our children need us to communicate with them about their problems and help them find a resolution. Too many parents, affronted when their children do not always take their advice or do what they want, then complain about them to their friends and neighbors. Gossiping about our children and their problems can only undermine their trust in us as parents. Things shared in confidence with us by our children should be kept in confidence. In the same way that the professional counselor protects the individuality of his or her client, a parent should guard the individuality and confidences of his or her children. If parents would talk more as adults and as equals with their children, their children would be less receptive to the control of peer groups. No teenager would choose his peers over his parents in a destructive way if his parents were parenting correctly. In the Motive Stage good parenting includes communication with your child as an adult equal and acknowledging and accepting the individuality of the child.

Goal of Stage

The goal of the Motive Stage is that adolescents, by the time they reach twenty, *become aware of the power of the inner self as they learn the meaning of human free will.* By the time a child reaches twenty, he or she is ready to leave childhood and dependency behind. In childhood, happiness was largely controlled by others, especially parents, and pain was caused by others. As an adult each person must learn that the meaning of human free will includes the reality that happiness is controlled by self and pain is largely something that we inflict on ourselves. For the adult, free will means that the primary control of one's satisfaction with life or suffering in life is determined by self. As was discussed earlier in this chapter, the process of utilizing free will and taking control of one's life is determined by our ability to understand our emotional states and the underlying motives within the heart that creates them. The importance of the parents' willingness to communicate with their children stems from this need for understanding the inner self. This means that dialogue between parents and teens will only be helpful if the parents are able through the dialogue to make the teens' inner self understandable.

This cannot be done unless the parents have already come to understand their own inner selves and then are willing to share them honestly with their teenagers. In other words, adolescents come to understand their own thoughts, feelings, and motives as adults are willing to share theirs with them. In the same way, adolescents learn how to deal with their own internal psychospiritual conflicts as the parents model successfully the resolution of problems in their own lives. This means that the parent who opens up his or her inner self and acknowledges weaknesses to his or her teenager will actually be perceived by that teenager as stronger. Strength is in being honest about self in front of teenagers rather than in trying to hide self from them.

In terms of free will, the reason parents need to give their children freedom during adolescence as the teens assume more responsibility is that at the end of adolescence they will stand free before God and become accountable to Him. In this way freedom and free will come to be associated with accountability and responsibility. Parents who withhold freedom and responsibility from their teenage children are depriving them of a necessary ingredient for happiness as adults. Many times children do not receive any freedom until they leave home, with the result being that they are overwhelmed by the freedom and, therefore, do not initially know how to use it responsibly. It is up to the parents to teach their teenagers that they have a free will and that as they leave home they will be accountable for themselves. This is the beginning of adult maturity.

PSYCHOLOGICAL NEED

Basic Need

In terms of our hierarchy of basic human needs, the primary need associated with the Motive Stage is *acceptance*. The teenager wants to feel that he or she belongs—the teenager wants to be a part of or included in a group. The only problem is that membership in the group centers around conformity to the group norms at the expense of individuality. The focus is upon what is the "in" thing to do. If it is "in" for boys to have long hair, then every male who does not want to be made fun of must have long hair. If it is "in" to wear blue jeans to school, then every child wants to wear blue jeans so they will not be different. If it is "in" to smoke marijuana or drink alcoholic beverages or be involved in premarital sex, then most teens will want to do these things so that they will not be thought of as "square." In this case "square" seemingly means old-fashioned, but actually it means not being willing to be controlled by the peer group.

For the teen to be different is to be singled out for special examination and treatment, mostly in the form of ridicule. Since no child likes to be made fun of, in most cases the ridicule eventually leads to conformity. From the teen's perspective, conformity means power, freedom, and acceptance. On the other hand, lack of conformity leads to attack and rejection. The teenage peer group and the fads that it creates have become a powerful force in our society, economically as well as psychologically. Millions of dollars are being made in the record and movie industries through the simple principle that teenagers like to herd together and do what everyone else is doing. Over the years specific fads come and go, but the control of the peer group remains. In the end one's acceptance is based on one's willingness to please others and conform to group standards. To base your acceptance upon doing only that which pleases others makes your self-esteem very vulnerable. Anytime someone does not like you, it undermines your self-esteem.

As a result, the need for acceptance cannot be met within the adolescent peer group. Although it takes a strong individual to stand up to the peer group during adolescence, it can be done. Those teenagers who resist peer control do so because they have strong, positive ties with their parents. To protect their teenagers from the dangers of the adolescent peer group, parents need to teach their children values and love them as individuals. Through open communication parents need to encourage their children over and over again to think for themselves and not to be afraid to say no if they feel something is wrong. This means that continued acceptance and love by their parents help teenagers through this difficult time of life.

However, even parental acceptance is not enough to meet the basic need for acceptance. The real goal is that by the time teens reach adulthood, they will have come to accept themselves. Too many teenagers are trying to become something they are not in order to please their friends and their parents. In the end, the need for acceptance is met when children can accept themselves just as they are without putting self down. Teens should be able to acknowledge that, whatever they are, God made them that way and He thinks they are beautiful and loves them. They need to learn to love themselves.

The positive emotion that results when the need for acceptance is met through self-acceptance is *hope*. Hope centers on the idea that *I am a valuable person to God and He feels my life can have significance—I am okay, I am normal, I have potential, I can be somebody.* For the teenager, control by the peer group destroys hope because it destroys individuality and self-worth. Having the inner strength and confidence to step out in life and be yourself and do what you want to do sets the teenager free from peer group control. This creates hope in the child. The emotion of hope, therefore, stems from the idea that in being myself I can do something meaningful with my life and control my future. This view allows the teenager to begin to look toward tomorrow with anticipation rather than dread, and the potential of life becomes exciting.

Psychological State

The psychological state associated with the Motive Stage is one of *independence/dependence*. According to the Bible, the child is to be considered a child and under the control and authority of the parents up through the teenage years. For this reason the child under this continued authority of parents is still in a state of dependence. Also, the teenager, although struggling hard to be autonomous, is not yet ready for total psychological separation from parents. In this way the child continues to be both spiritually and psychologically dependent upon his or her parents. Note, however, that the term *dependence* is listed second and the term *independence* is listed first. Although a state of dependency still exists in relation to the parents, it is not to be considered primary. Parents who try to keep their teen in a primary state of dependence create psychological problems in the child and conflict in the family. Children respond to this attempt to keep them dependent in one of two ways. Some children cope with this dependency by blocking their emotional development through becoming shy, passive, and insecure. Other teens rebel against their parents' authority. Either way there will be problems.

Parents need to make sure that they spend more time reflecting independence than dependence to their teenager. This is done by giving the child responsibility and the freedom to make choices. It is still acceptable for parents to have limits for their children, (for example, a curfew for dating), but these limits should be flexible. What is most important is that the child begins to think of him- or herself as an individual with a free will who must become responsible for what he or she is and what he or she does. When the child makes a mistake, the parents need to help the child face the consequences, not help him or her escape them. In adolescence, therefore, positive psychological development depends upon whether or not the parents allow the child greater independence and help him or her develop greater maturity of judgment.

Self-Esteem

The self-esteem of teenagers stems out of how well the need for acceptance has been met. The issue is one of learning to like oneself. Initially teens try to like self through being liked by others. They seek the acceptance and approval of others as the basis for determining their own worth and value. The problem with this is that other people, like self, are basically egocentric. As a result other people also have a need for acceptance and approval. In this way, all teenagers are seeking to get from others the acceptance they crave, but no one is really able to give it, especially when it comes to love.

In this stage love is something that every teen is trying to get from other teens. This is like the blind leading the blind. Through their egocentric orientation, all teens want to be loved but no one in the peer group really knows how to give love. As adults, love does not begin as we obtain it from others, but as we obtain it from God. The beginning of love in our lives stems from the fact that God loved us and sent His son to die for us on the cross. Self-love starts when we can begin to see ourselves the way God does. On the one hand, our works mean less to Him than we think they do, but on the other, we mean more. Self-esteem comes in this stage when we can *learn to like ourselves just the way God made us.*

HUMAN FALL

Again, as in the previous stages, no child will come through the Motive Stage without being marred by sin. In the struggles during the teen years between the parents and child and between the child and his or her peers mistakes will be made and the child will be hurt. However, the child is now old enough to also hurt back. In this stage negative emotions and evil motives begin to develop and the child can now hurt her parents as much as she feels they have hurt her. What the child eventually learns, however, is that the satisfaction associated with hurting others is not lasting and it never eliminates the pain and suffering that continues inside self.

Negative Cognitive States

Two negative cognitive states arise during the Motive Stage that are used as defenses when the need for acceptance is not met. The first of these is *loneliness*. Probably the most pervading state experienced by teenagers, loneliness is usually never recognized and labeled, so most teens are not aware of its existence. However, the loneliness is real and it gnaws constantly at the insides. Loneliness runs through much of the music listened to by teens. Most of these songs have something to do with love—finding it, losing it, seeking it. In this way, teenagers' search for love is really an attempt to overcome loneliness. The problem is that nothing seems to work. Teenagers attempt to use sex as a substitute for love, but only feel more lonely after the sex is over. The next step is to try and hide the loneliness through parties, drugs, and alcohol. But the party always ends and the drug's effects eventually wear off and the loneliness always remains. The negative emotional state that stems from loneliness is one of *envy,* or jealousy. Because of basic egocentrism, all teenagers think that they are the only ones with the problem of loneliness. In other words, they look at other teens who seem to be getting attention—the good student, the good athlete, the pretty girl—and assume that because they have these attributes they are not lonely. As a result, they become envious of them. The neurotic thinking here is that if I could just be like them I would also get more attention and then I would not be lonely any more. What these envious teens do not realize is that all teens are lonely, even the popular ones. The problem is universal. The problem of loneliness, though, does not stem from our lack of acceptance by others, but is a true existential state arising from our separation from God and His love. *Human love does not have the capacity to help us overcome the state of loneliness.*

The second negative cognitive state associated with the Motive Stage is *boredom.* In this case, boredom is merely a defense against loneliness. The teen who always talks about being bored is trying to repress his or her loneliness and hide it from self and others. The person who focuses on the state of loneliness places the blame for the problem on him- or herself—i.e., if I could be this or do this then people would like me. The person who is in a state of boredom, however, is blaming his or her feelings of loneliness on others. The primary focal point of this attack is on parents and other adults as authority figures. The bored child also places the blame for unhappiness in life on others. He or she seeks constant highs, and when they are not forthcoming he or she gets bored. The negative emotional state associated with boredom is *hatred.* As we examine our young people today, we find more and more of them who are bored. The deeper this boredom becomes, the more hatred and violence we see. These teenagers are striking back at parents and a society that they feel has neglected them. In most cases bored children were spoiled by the parents during earlier stages. They were not disciplined enough, they were given too many things, and they did not receive enough love. As a result, such teenagers have not learned how to cope with frustration. Boredom, then, arises in a teenager who down deep feels lonely while also feeling frustrated and deprived and is looking for someone to blame it on and attack.

Primary Fear

The primary fear, therefore, associated with the Motive Stage is the fear of *rejection*. The potential for rejection is daily in a teenager's life. One can be rejected by parents, one can be rejected by teachers, and one can be rejected by friends. When one's need for acceptance depends upon what others think, it only takes one mistake a day to become rejected by someone. In most cases this one rejection is then overgeneralized to the point that if one person, any person, does not like me then I must be unlikeable. In this context, the fear of rejection continually becomes a reality for most teenagers since it only takes one bad reflection to wipe out ninety-nine good ones. In the Behavior Stage the focus was on doing bad things, now it is on being a bad person with the assumption that if I am a bad person no one will like me. This is why the teenager is very sensitive to any criticism. Parents may see criticism as an attack on the child's behavior, but children see it as an attack on them.

Existential Sin

The existential sin that stems from the teenager's fear of rejection, and eventually makes it worse, is the sin of *inferiority*. Through the fear of rejection by others, every teenager develops the sin of inferiority. Inferiority undermines self-esteem and blocks the ability to become a success in life, keeping the child from moving on to adulthood and taking the risks necessary to contribute to society in a positive way. But even more important, the sin of inferiority blocks a person's ability to love and be loved. The inferior person believes down deep that nobody loves him or her because he or she does not have anything to offer others that is worthy of love. The person in the sin of inferiority denies his or her talents and shirks his or her duty in the name of suffering. Inferiority causes one to be a pessimist about life and tries to call attention to how much one is suffering. Inferiority causes one to make a virtue out of being miserable. The neurotic fantasy associated with the sin of inferiority is that *I am so worthless or bad that no one could like me.*

The usual result of this psychological ploy is that it brings sympathy and encouragement from others and gives the person the attention he or she craves. In the end, although the sin of inferiority brings attention, it does not bring self-esteem and the person is left in a state of unhappiness. The sin of inferiority also denies God's Word when it tells us that we were created by God and that we do have worth. To make ourselves worthless is to make Christ's sacrifice meaningless.

MOTIVE STAGE

Human Responsibility	
Primary Responsibility	**Adults as models**
Major Task	To help children feel like they are becoming a normal adult.
Technique	**Open communication as equals**
Focal Point	**Talk with**
Goal	To become aware of the inner self and the meaning of free will.
Psychological Need	
Basic Need	**Acceptance**
Resultant Positive Emotion	**Hope**
Psychological State	**Independence/Dependence**
Self-Esteem	I must **like** myself just the way God made me.
Human Fall	
Negative Cognitive Stages	**Loneliness** **Boredom**
Resultant Negative Emotions	↓ **Envy** ↓ **Hatred**
Primary Fear	**Rejection**
Existential Sin	**Inferiority**
Neurotic Fantasy	I am so worthless or bad that no one could like me.

8

The Unstage

The Unstage can be thought of as the *crossroads of life*. It is the transition point between childhood and adulthood and stands between the Motive Stage and the Meaning Stage.

The Unstage ranges from approximately fifteen to twenty-five years of age, with the primary focus on the years from eighteen through twenty-two. This means that the Unstage overlaps with the stage preceding it as well as the stage following it. The reality of the Unstage acknowledges that the transition from childhood to adulthood is neither an easy transition nor immediate. It takes time for young adults to separate emotionally from their parents as they move on to the adult state of independence. For some, this process flows smoothly without major conflicts, but for many others it is a time fraught with insecurity and conflict.

The Unstage involves much more than just physical separation of the young adult from home and parents. There are many young people who have their own job, house, and/or marriage and yet remain in the Unstage. The Unstage is not completed until young adults have established psychospiritual independence. This means that they must be able to let go of childhood, psychologically and spiritually, as they assume adult responsibilities in all areas of their lives. This principle is taught in I Corinthians 13:11, which states: "When I was a child, I spoke as a child, I understood as a child, I thought as a child: but when I became a man, I put away childish things."

Most young people have been misled as to the true nature of independence. Today independence has been equated with liberty or freedom, which was the primary need of the Obedience Stage. Most young adults feel that freedom and independence are synonymous terms. To be independent, therefore, has come to be defined as coming to a point in your life where you are free to do whatever you want; to go where you want to go, to stay out as late as you want to stay, to eat what you want to eat, and to put into your body whatever you want to put into it (i.e., drugs and alcohol). The young person associates becoming an adult with the freedom to do whatever he desires. The fantasy is that *once I break free from parental authority, there will be no more authority, no more limits, and no more control on my life; I can now do whatever I please.* In this way, independence has come to be defined as an escape from authority and limits.

By defining independence as freedom from authority and limits, we create the problem of a rebellious young adult. Today's society has the warped idea that the more rebellious the young adult is the more independent he or she is becoming. This means that not only is independence wrongly tied to the issue of freedom, this definition of freedom can only be obtained through rebellion. As a result, more and more young people rebel more and more against parental and social authority in the name of reaching adulthood and independence. This idea is being reinforced by secular social scientists who also define adulthood in terms of autonomy of self and freedom to do your own thing.

In the chapter on the Obedience Stage it was established that liberty or freedom should be dealt with as a primary need between the ages of two and six. The conflict over the definition of freedom was resolved from a Christian perspective in that true freedom only comes as one learns to live within limits and under authority. We rejected the secular humanistic view that freedom could be defined as the ability to live outside limits and outside the control of authority, because all authority stems from God and no one can escape God's authority, whether it is direct or delegated. Therefore, the focus of the young adult on freedom leading to rebellion is not a step forward toward adulthood, but actually a regressive step toward the Obedience Stage of childhood. Rebellion is not a psychological state associated with the true maturity of adulthood, but is actually a sign of continued immaturity.

Young adults who decide to remain dependent on their parents and others for their security and self-esteem have become fixated in their development. For an adult always to do what others want or tell him or her to do is immature and inappropriate and a sign that psychologically that person is still a child. We call this state of continued dependency in someone who is by age an adult the state of *adaptive child*. On the other hand, the young adult who needs to rebel against parents and other authority figures in order to have self-worth is also in a continued state of immaturity. Always to need to do the opposite of what authority dictates makes one just as much controlled by that authority as the person who always needs to follow it. This means that rebellion does not lead to freedom, but merely to a new form of control. In reality, the rebellious young adult actually remains dependent on the very people that he or she tries so hard to rebel against. We call this the state of *rebellious child*.

The adaptive child and the rebellious child states as found in young adults are still both states of dependency. To be in either of these states in the Unstage eventually leads to emotional regression, and the person begins to move backward in their psychospiritual development.

If rebellion and freedom are not goals of independence, the next question is, what are? The primary term that needs to be associated with the true state of independence is the word *responsibility*. Becoming a mature adult stems from the assuming of responsibilities rather than the obtaining of privileges. Today too many young people have been raised thinking of life as a free ride. When one becomes an adult and leaves the protection of parents behind, nothing is free anymore. The adult gets out of life what he or she is willing to put into it. Young people want instant everything today: instant happiness, instant love, instant pleasure, instant satisfaction of needs. The focus has been switched from giving to taking, and in this way we are becoming a bankrupt society in all areas of our life. We are becoming bankrupt economically because people want to spend more than they work (earn). We are becoming bankrupt in marriage because people want to take more love out of a marriage than they are willing to put into it. We are becoming bankrupt in our families because children as takers become a curse rather than a blessing as they compete with the selfish needs of the parents. We are becoming bankrupt psychologically because we want happiness without stress (pain). Finally, we are becoming bankrupt spiritually because we want the blessings of God without having to make a commitment to Him. In all of these areas the focus has been shifted from contributing to our society to getting for self.

True independence and responsibility are brought together in the Bible in the parable of the prodigal son. This parable, found in Luke 15:11–32, clearly presents the truths that we have been discussing concerning the Unstage and the meaning of independence. The first half of the story involves the younger of two sons who went to his father and asked for his inheritance. He took this inheritance and went to the big city, where he spent it all having a good time. Without financial resources, he was deserted by his so-called friends and ended up working as a hired hand for a farmer. One day he decided to return home in humility to his father and admit his folly and immaturity. In doing this the father welcomed him home. The second half of the story involves the older son who remained at home. It deals with this son's jealousy toward the younger son when he returned home.

In this parable the two sons represent the two childhood states that one can carry into adulthood. The prodigal son represents the rebellious child state and the older son represents the adaptive child state. The younger son associated being grownup with pleasure and having a good time. Eventually, he came to see that rebellion was a deadend strategy. In coming home he was willing to be a servant, which meant that he now understood that adulthood involved work and the taking on of responsibilities. The older son stayed at home and worked. However, he worked to please his father. In this way he was associating doing one's duty with being acceptable to his father. What he did not understand was that his father's acceptance of his sons was not determined by what they did, but what they were—sons. As a result, the older son became jealous and angry and did not rejoice when the younger son returned. The story concludes before we ever find out the fate of the older son and whether he was able to break out of the adaptive child state and reach true independence.

The Unstage, therefore, represents the crossroads of life. The responsibility for self needs to be shifted from parents to the young adult. In today's society this process is not an easy one for our young people because we have allowed secular humanistic educators and social scientists to define wrongly the meaning of independence as freedom. The Christian view as established in the Bible is that adulthood and maturity are based on the taking on of responsibilities rather than the obtaining of privileges. For life to take on meaning, the young adult must learn that lasting happiness only comes from giving of self rather than getting for self.

THE EXODUS ANALOGY

In the Bible the book of Exodus tells the true historical story of how God used Moses to lead God's chosen people from slavery under Pharaoh in Egypt through the wilderness to the land of Canaan which He had promised them. In terms of our developmental stages, the Unstage can best be explained and understood through the use of the story of the exodus of the Jews.

In our analogy, Egypt represents childhood, the wilderness represents the Unstage, and the Promised Land represents adulthood. When Joseph first had his family brought to Egypt, they were not slaves but free men. In the same way we should not consider the four stages of childhood as stages of slavery, but stages of freedom. At each stage of childhood the child should be viewed as a child and treated like a child. In other words, children should be expected to act and think like children within the developmental sequence. This means that we should expect babies to be egocentric and preschoolers to be rebellious. These problems of childhood are not to be overcome through a supernatural act of God, but through the effort and faithfulness of parents. There comes a time in every person's life, however, when childhood must be left behind. The only exception to this is for those people who are so severely retarded that they never progress beyond the stages of childhood.

To try to hold on to childish ways of acting, thinking, and feeling after childhood is over is to enter a state of psychospiritual slavery. Adults who are still trying to be children are in bondage and need to be set free. In this case the bondage is not to Pharaoh, but to Satan. Those adults who do not reach true independence because they do not face and resolve childhood developmental fixations and conflicts will eventually come under the control of Satan, who will play on their vulnerabilities as he leads them to sin. As the young adult moves from childhood to adulthood, he or she enters into a spiritual warfare taking place between God and Satan. To be independent is to be free to choose. The question for those in the Unstage concerns what choices should be made and why. Who is it that the person is going to follow—God or Satan?

As Christians, we have failed in making sure that each young person understands the importance and ramifications of this choice. Humanistic psychology makes self the highest state and in so doing self becomes god. The assumption is that self is basically good, and when choices are made they will naturally lead to self-actualization. The hope is that as people self-actualize the good within them, human beings will come together in love and create a world of peace. In this way, man will have recreated the Garden of Eden, this time without God, and he will live there forever with no sin and no judgment. This may be a nice plot for a fairytale, but it cannot stand up to the test of reality. Reality shows us that as man rejects God he does not get more love, but less; and as man rejects God he does not get more peace, but more war.

The choice of the Unstage has come to be one between self, which has been judged by the secular humanists to be good, and religion, which has been attacked by the secular humanists as outdated or bad. As a result, young adults are deceived as they choose self over religion as the primary source of happiness. In reality, it is not religion that is rejected, but God, and to reject God is to enter a state of sin. To be in a state of sin is to be in bondage to sin, or a slave to sin. To be a slave to sin is to allow oneself to be under the authority of Pharaoh or, in this case, Satan. In other words, to reject God as our authority is to choose Satan as our authority. This means that the choice is not really between self and God, as secular psychologists try to tell us, but between God and Satan. The spiritual battleground over this choice takes place in the wilderness that is the Unstage of life. The question centers around who will be put on the throne of one's life when parents are taken off. The following diagram illustrates the two alternatives we are faced with:

SECULAR HUMANISM   BIBLICAL CHRISTIANITY

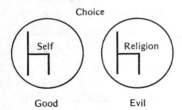
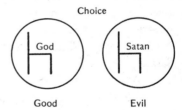

From our earlier discussion on the true meaning of independence, we can now clearly see that both the adaptive child state and the rebellious child state are states of slavery or bondage, and those young adults who remain in these states are in Egypt. The longer that a person stays in Egypt after he or she reaches adulthood, the more psychological problems will begin to develop in his or her life. Continued psychospiritual development during the Unstage is based on the person's willingness to cast off or let go of childhood and enter the wilderness. Most young adults want to jump from Egypt to the Promised Land without going through the wilderness. This is just not possible; you cannot get to the promised land of adulthood without going through the wilderness of the Unstage.

As the adaptive and rebellious child states are associated with slavery and Egypt, the wilderness is associated with the state of the *searching child*. To enter the wilderness, one must take the risk of stepping out in faith to find one's identity and purpose in life. The searching child cannot begin this quest for a unique identity and purpose until he or she is willing to acknowledge his or her own fallibility and imperfection. To reach adulthood one must grow, and to grow one must experience pain. The primary pain here is not physical, but emotional. To grow up, one must let go of childhood, but this cannot be done until one is willing to re-examine what took place there and resolve any conflicts that might remain. To enter the wilderness, therefore, is not to find one's future but to be willing to look at one's past. Until we can understand what we are, it will be impossible to control what we will become. In this way one cannot go on to adulthood at the crossroads of life until he or she first goes back to childhood by choice and examines the forces that are controlling his or her life. The Unstage, therefore, is a searching stage and the primary search is inside one's head.

As one begins to search one's past inside one's own head the reality of fallibility and imperfection will be established as the sin that exists in our memories is rediscovered. This sin comes from three sources—self, others, and environment. People on their own find the task of examining the sin in their lives too painful to complete. The primary reason for this is that in our humanity there is no escape from our sin. This is why secular counseling has failed. It can bring people to an awareness of their sin and the guilt associated with it, but cannot relieve them of the pain. In other words, counseling techniques that are only able to help people remember past sin in self, others, or environment only make people feel worse in the long run.

As Christians, we have a solution to this problem through the blood of Jesus Christ. People can be relieved from the guilt and pain associated with the sin that took place in their lives as children through the forgiveness of God obtained through the sacrificial atonement of Jesus Christ on the cross. Jesus Christ died on the cross to pay the price for our sin so that through God's forgiveness we can be set free from our bondage to the sin in our childhood. Crossing the Red Sea represents the power to cleanse and forgive us of sin that we obtain from our belief in Jesus Christ as our Savior. The Red Sea represents the blood of Christ that swallows up our sin and gives us the potential power to overcome Satan.

Coming under the blood of Christ should take place before we begin our search for self in the wilderness. Otherwise, the search will be too painful and we will eventually retreat back to Egypt. It is the painfulness associated with the sins in our memories that Satan uses to keep us in bondage. Jesus Christ wants to set us free from this slavery to sin so that our life can eventually take on purpose and meaning.

THE WILDERNESS EXPERIENCE

To be in the Unstage of life is a frightening experience. To be in the wilderness is to be like Christopher Columbus, who left the safety of the homeland shores and ventured out on to unchartered waters in hope of finding a new world. In the same way, young adults must leave the safety of home behind and set out on the sea of life with the hope that they will find a purpose or meaning for existence. Lack of certainty as to the dangers involved in the passage and what one will find on the other side of the wilderness leads to fear. Can I survive the wilderness without losing my sanity? Is there really a promised land? How do I really know that the promised land will be better than Egypt? Is it worth the pain involved to try and cross the wilderness? What's so bad about Egypt anyway? All of these questions in the mind of young adults work to make this period of life one of confusion and uncertainty. We will now look at four steps that must be taken in order to cross the wilderness.

Finding Self

Earlier in this chapter it was stated that humanists advocate choosing self over religion. This, however, assumes that one truly knows self. The young adult cannot know self until he or she discovers self and cannot discover self until he or she is willing to search honestly. Humanistic psychologists suggest that this search will be an easy one, and one that is fun, because human nature is basically good and, therefore, our search of our inner self will find basically good things. The Christian view is just the opposite. The Bible teaches that, although man is created in God's image, through the fall man is in a state of sin. As a result, there is a sinful nature within each one of us that is evil and that in our humanity always seems to overwhelm the good that we desire to do. The Christian view is that the wilderness search for our inner self will be a difficult one, and one that is painful, since much of what we find as we examine our motives and emotions will be evil and ugly. The conclusion drawn is that we cannot develop our inner beauty until we first discover and deal with our inner ugliness.

During the Motive Stage the adolescent begins to see and understand the ugliness and imperfections of others, especially of parents. The teen uses this insight as a weapon to make people, especially authority figures, back off by pointing out their flaws. One of the reasons there is so much conformity among adolescents is that to be yourself is to show your flaws, which makes you vulnerable to attack by your peers. As a result, teenagers try to protect themselves from attack by developing a facade or mask behind which they hide. From the perspective of the teen it is okay to point out and attack the flaws in others, but it is unacceptable to be attacked in return.

Most teenagers during the Motive Stage become much better at understanding the true motives and feelings of others than they do at understanding themselves. The wilderness experience in the Unstage requires that the young adult drop the facade, at least in relation to self, and look behind the mask. This may sound strange, but our conclusion is that young adults, as well as many older adults, do not know who they really are; they do not know what is behind the mask and they are afraid to take it off and look.

When the mask is finally removed, the worst fears will be confirmed. When we begin to examine our hearts for our hidden motives and emotional states, what we find will not be pretty. Sitting there will be all of the deadwood left over from the marring that took place in each of the four childhood stages. We will find the sins of egocentrism, rebellion, pride, and inferiority. We will find unresolved negative feelings of anxiety, frustration, fear, anger, shame, conceit, envy, and hatred. We will experience the negative cognitive states of separation, deprivation, helplessness, weakness, failure, superiority, loneliness, and boredom. We will experience the primary fears of abandonment, punishment, disapproval, and rejection. Finally, we will have to face and deal with our neurotic fantasies. Needless to say, the wilderness cannot be crossed quickly. It will take time to become aware of the full power that sin has had on our lives and the scars that it has left.

When faced with the full extent of his own depravity, the initial response of a fallen man is to look for someone else to blame it on. Adam and Eve both used this technique. As a result, we can expect young adults to initially look for someone to blame for the evil that exists within them. The most common scapegoat used is parents. It is true that the parents as sinners contributed to the imperfections that exist within our inner self. However, we already discussed that the sin within us comes from three sources—self, others, and environment. After the fall the earth and every living creature on it, including man, was affected by it. This means that sin is inevitable and there is no escape from it. If the parents failed to raise a child perfectly, it was only because perfect parenting was an impossibility within an imperfect parent. The question I raise when counseling college students who are struggling with this problem concerns their rationale for condemning their parents for being imperfect. If imperfection is the state of all human beings, how could their parents be anything but imperfect? An adult's psychological problems are not caused by the mistakes of imperfect parents, because everyone had imperfect parents. In most cases, the parents only did their best in relation to what they started with in terms of the deficiencies that they experienced in their childhood.

As a result, blaming others, and especially our parents, for the flaws we find in the hidden man of our heart merely dooms us to wander in circles in the wilderness until we die. No one ever got out of the wilderness and found the promised land of psychospiritual happiness by blaming their problems on others. This leads us to the second step of our wilderness journey.

Assume Control

The second step centers around defining the full meaning of the implications involved in having a free will. To have human free will means that one can choose and, through those choices, control one's destiny. Once obtained, free will can never be given away. Man standing before God with the freedom to choose must also acknowledge that he will be responsible and accountable for the choices that he makes. This is what the young adult in the wilderness must come to see—to enter the promised land requires that he or she must choose to assume control of his or her own life through an acknowledgment of free will. Most people only want to admit free will in relation to the good that is in them or the good that happens to them, but always want to blame the evil on someone or something else. The statement "You made me angry" is a clear example of an attempt to deny one's free will. To assume control of one's life as an adult, it is necessary to take full responsibility for all of one's motives, emotional states, and behaviors.

During childhood the child is instructed to obey his or her parents. As the child fulfills this injunction to obey, the parents become accountable for what the child is asked to be and do. To leave childhood behind, however, it becomes necessary for the young adult to leave parental authority and begin to think, feel, and choose for self. The young adult who continues to live under parental authority or other human authority figures denies his or her human free will. This allows the person to blame others for life's failures and personal unhappiness. While in the short run this may seem to the person to be the easiest way to get through life, in the long run it places the fate of one's happiness in the hands of others. This does not fit in with the teachings of Scripture. The Bible teaches that every person will someday have to stand and give an accounting of his or her life before God. It also teaches that each person is responsible for his or her own sin, which must be dealt with individually. To assume control, therefore, is to acknowledge one's free will and, thereby, affirm that what I am and what I become is determined by me.

Internalize Values

After one is willing to assume personal responsibility for one's psychospiritual health, he or she is ready to take the third step in the wilderness. This step involves the changing of one's beliefs and values from an external locus of control to an internal locus of control. During childhood, values and beliefs were learned and followed on the basis of an external, extrinsic value system incorporated from human authority figures who were perceived as omnipotent. To assume free will means that the young adult must let go of human authority figures as omnipotent forces in one's life and learn to choose for self. During this wilderness experience, young adults begin to examine personally the values and beliefs taught and enforced by their parents to see if they are really worth retaining. This is a very difficult time for the parents when the child begins to question their values and beliefs.

The danger associated with this examination of values is that the person might reject values that are good and learn new ones that are bad. The problem for the young adult during this values clarification period concerns the standard that is to be used to judge whether certain values and beliefs are good or bad. One thing that young people cannot tolerate during this time of questioning values is hypocrisy. Hypocrisy simply means that the authority figure teaches one set of values but actually lives by another. The young adult finds it easier to evaluate values and beliefs if his or her parents show consistency in relation to what they say and do.

We must admit that there is a real crisis of values in our country today. Parents and other authority figures, including the church, seem to have lost much of their credibility due to an inconsistency that has developed between the values being taught and those being lived. As a result, most young people today seem confused in their task of trying to establish an internal value system.

The question in their minds concerns what is to be the base of values if parents and authority cannot be trusted. The result has been that more and more young people are living by a relative value system based on a pleasure principle that shifts from day to day according to whim or impulse. In our modern society, no one seems to be able to find any values that are lasting anymore. This is because we have left God out of the process.

The source of lasting values and beliefs needs to be God and His Word. For young adults to establish an internal, intrinsic value system that is able to meet their inner needs, they must turn to an omnipotent God for the guidelines. As Christians, we must reaffirm that there are absolute values, morals, and beliefs established by God, and these principles must be followed in order to find happiness and psychospiritual health.

Finish Childhood

The final step in the journey through the wilderness is the most important. Before any person can go on to mature adulthood, it is essential to resolve the negative conflicts that remain from childhood. This means that a person must go back to the Nurturance Stage and work his or her way back up through the four childhood stages as an adult, dealing with all of the negative emotional states, cognitive states, fears, and sins that remain. In most cases, each person will find that some stages are more difficult to complete than others. This process of finishing childhood must be viewed as idiosyncratic; it will be different for every person, even brothers and sisters raised in the same home. Where there are sins, they must be confessed. Where there scars, they must be healed. Where there is low self-esteem and inferiority, there must be self-confidence. Where there is emotional weakness and vulnerability, there must be strength and courage. No one ever really goes on to the adult stages of life and deals with them successfully until he or she first goes back and psychologically and spiritually reconstructs his or her childhood. In doing this, God must replace parents as the primary seat of interaction. We need to place our security in God; we need to find our liberty within God's authority; we need to be competent by following God's commands; and we need to find acceptance from God through believing in Jesus Christ as our Savior. Once we do this, we are ready to enter the promised land.

CROSSING THE JORDAN

From the Exodus story we find that to make it through the wilderness is not enough to get us into the promised land. The people of Israel wavered at the point of reaching their goal. Of the twelve spies sent out, only two were willing to go on. The people sided with the ten and rejected God's plan. As a result, they were judged by God and made to wander in the wilderness until they died. Only Joshua and Caleb and the children were allowed to enter the land. In another Bible story Lot's wife when leaving Sodom also wavered and looked back and was turned into a pillar of salt. The point is that the Bible is full of stories in which people made it to the Jordan but never got across. What is it then that allows a person in the psychospiritual developmental process to cross over the Jordan and, thereby, complete the Unstage? *Commitment.* It is possible in our wanderings and searchings for our identity and meaning in life to confront the reality of God as a possible solution. However, we cannot obtain God's promises without first making a commitment to Him. This commitment is one that must be made by self out of free will based upon an intrinsic belief system. This commitment must be made by the heart and not just the mind. Finally, this commitment must be total.

When faced with the demand for total commitment to the cause, most people hesitate. Standing on the edge of the Jordan, the young adult is faced with three choices: 1) go back to Egypt, 2) continue to wander in the wilderness with the hope that maybe there will be another promised land better than this one, or 3) go in and possess the land. Sad to say, most people end the Unstage by making either the first or second choices. Very few choose to go all the way. To go all the way requires that we choose the cause over our possessions. To go all the way means that the cause must be more important than our life in that we are willing to sacrifice life itself if that is what it takes. To go all the way means that the cause must be more important than our friends in that we are willing to forsake them because of it. Needless to say, very few people are willing to make this kind of sacrifice. Like Lot's wife, we have become too much a part of this world to be willing to let go totally and leave it behind.

For the Christian, crossing the Jordan River centers around Christ's resurrection. Jesus died as our Savior as represented by the blood and the Red Sea, but he arose victoriously as our Lord as represented by the Jordan River. To cross the Jordan River and get to the promised land requires that we commit ourselves to the Lordship of Christ. Through his death and resurrection, the promised land now belongs to Jesus and the Bible says that the entrance is narrow and few people find it. To move on successfully to the psychospiritual stages of adulthood requires that young adults do more than just put Christ in their lives; they must put Christ on the throne of their lives. Until Christ is Lord of our life, we will never be allowed to enter the promised land. The following chart outlines what we have been discussing in this chapter.

CROSSROADS OF LIFE

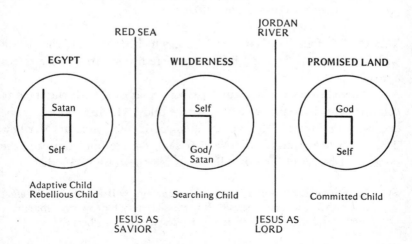

The importance of a commitment to the Lordship of Christ is presented in the Bible. That few people find the promised land is verified in Matthew 7:13, where it says:

> Enter ye in at the straight gate, for wide is the gate and broad is the way that leads to destruction and many there be which go in there. Because straight is the gate and narrow is the way which leadeth unto life and few there be that find it.

The narrow way into the promised land is also afirmed in Matthew 7:21, as it tells us:

> Not every one that says unto me Lord, Lord shall enter into the kingdom of heaven, but he that doeth the will of my Father which is in heaven. Many will say to me in that day Lord, Lord have we not . . . . And then I will profess unto them, I never knew you, depart from me, ye that work iniquity.

The idea that a choice as to who will be on the throne of one's life must be made is found in Matthew 6:24, where it states:

> No man can serve two masters: for either he will hate the one and love the other or else he will hold to the one and despise the other. You cannot serve God and man (self).

This truth is found in Matthew 12:30, which states, "He that is not with me is against me and he that gathereth not with me scattereth abroad."

There are several scriptural passages that deal with the issue of commitment. In Matthew 10:22, we are told, "He that endures to the end shall be saved." This same statement is also found in Matthew 24:13, where it states, "But he that shall endure unto the end, the same shall be saved." Jesus tells us in Matthew 10:32,33 that:

> Whosoever shall confess me before men, him will I confess also before my Father which is in heaven. But whosoever shall deny me before men, him will I also deny before my Father which is in heaven."

Finally, Jesus demands total commitment in Matthew 10: 38,39 when He states, "And he that taketh not his cross and followeth after me is not worthy of me. He that findeth his life shall lose it: and he that loseth his life for my sake shall find it." This is repeated in Matthew 16:24-26:

> If any man will come after me let him deny himself and take up his cross and follow me. For whosoever will save his life shall lose it: and whosoever will lose his life for my sake shall find it. For what is a man profited if he shall gain the whole world and lost his own soul?"

We must help people to see that the sovereignty of God and the Lordship of Christ are not potential realities but true realities. God *is* sovereign and Christ *is* Lord, regardless of what men think, do, or say. God gave man a free will to choose which He will not destroy, but He will surely judge each one of us on the basis of the choices we have made. One day we will all stand accountable before God and God alone. This was established first in the Ten Commandments when God said in Exodus 20:2,3: "I am the Lord thy God . . . Thou shalt have no other gods before me."

This demand for total commitment by God was continued through Jesus Christ as presented in Philippians 2:9–11,

> Wherefore God also hath highly exalted him and given him a name which is above every other name: That at the name of Jesus every knee should bow . . . and that every tongue should confess that Jesus is Lord to the glory of God the Father.

Through Christ's death and resurrection, we will all stand accountable as reflected in Romans 14:10–12,

> We shall all stand before the judgment seat of Christ. For it is written, As I live, saith the Lord, every knee shall bow to me and every tongue shall confess to God. So then every one of us shall give account of himself to God.

	EGYPT	WILDERNESS	PROMISED LAND
1. Religious Behaviors (Tithing, Prayer, Bible Study, Church Attendance)	1. Reasoning • Should do it • Must do it • Good Christians do it • Feel guilty if I don't	1. Reasoning If you do not get anything out of an activity, there is no sense in doing it. Involvement is sporadic. Sometimes it's meaningful, sometimes not.	1. Reasoning I do these things because I want to, because they are meaningful, because they stem from a real relationship with God.
2. Ethical Questions	2. Reasoning Absolute concepts of right and wrong arbitrarily applied. Person is told what to do by an authority figure. (Adultery as an act is always a sin.)	2. Reasoning Authority figures are just human beings who also can make mistakes, must learn to think for self. Concepts of right and wrong relative to each individual. (There may be times when adultery as an act is not a sin in terms of the higher law of love.)	2. Reasoning There are absolute concepts of right and wrong but they cannot be arbitrarily imposed. The standard is the individual conscience standing before God accountable for self based on what is in the heart. (Adultery is always a sin. There are times when a person who has not committed the act of adultery has committed the sin of adultery.)

		3.	4.
3.	God's Will	What does God want me to do? (Marriage, job, college major) If I make the right choice, life will be easy.	It is not always clear what God wants me to do. Sometimes He seems so far away. If you cannot see clearly what God wants you to do you just have to do what you think is best.	The reason people cannot figure out what God wants them to do is that they have stopped growing. God's will is more related to our being— becoming than our doing. If we are becoming what God wants us to be, the doing will take care of itself.
4.	Psychological Security	Security in external, extrinsic value system incorporated from human authority figures perceived as omnipotent	Insecurity due to an inability to distinguish between extrinsic and intrinsic values. Cannot see that one does not have to reject values because the person teaching them is not omnipotent. Value system becomes relative guided by human reasoning.	Security in an internal, intrinsic value system derived from a personal relationship to an omnipotent God.

Since one day we will all be judged by God through the Lordship of Christ, it is important that we discern just where we are. We need to look and see whether we are in Egypt, in the wilderness, or in the promised land. Many of the people in our churches today neither are living victorious Christian lives nor have entered the promised land in terms of the psychospiritual developmental stages. Many do not even know how to go about evaluating their spiritual state. The following chart was constructed to allow those who are seeking to be Christians to evaluate their lives in order to identify where they are presently located. The hope is that all those who read this chapter will finally stop trying to hold on to control of their own lives and go all the way to total commitment to the cause of Christ. It is the only choice that can be made in the Unstage that will lead to true happiness in one's search for meaning in the next stage.

9
Meaning Stage

The Meaning Stage runs from age twenty to age thirty and is associated with defining the meaning of the Lordship of Christ. The main struggle centers around a quest for meaning and purpose in one's life. Relevant questions include: Why am I here? What am I to be? Where should I go? In the Meaning Stage each person is seeking his or her own destiny and fulfillment. To become a totally committed Christian sold out to the cause of Christ does not immediately tell one what major to choose in college, what vocation to go into, what person to marry, or where to live. Meaning for the Christian centers around how to go about discerning the will of God in life's choices. Although the Bible tells us that God does have a plan for our life, in reality He never seems to come right out and audibly tell us what to do. In other words, we ourselves are still left with the need to make the choices, and there are no guarantees that the choices we make really will be those which God wanted. Even as a Christian under the Lordship of Christ, we still must deal with human free will. We will continue to have to deal with the reality of sin in our life. To make Christ Lord merely gives us the power to overcome sin and the sinful nature within us, but we still must choose to use that power.

Psychospiritual development, therefore, does not stop when we become an adult, it merely moves on to a new stage with new challenges and new pitfalls. People who do not turn to God to find a purpose for their lives during the Meaning Stage begin to experience a state we will call a *crisis of meaning*. In the crisis of meaning, persons find themselves drifting through life with no apparent purpose or direction. For most people, this crisis of meaning produces too much anxiety, so they look for a substitute source of meaning other than through God's will. The primary substitute used by fallen man is social roles.

Throughout history the male has traditionally attempted to define meaning and purpose in terms of his work role, the job through which he attempts to provide for his family's needs. When asked what they are, most adult men answer in terms of the defined work role they play in society—I am a doctor, I am a teacher, I am a truck driver, I am a farmer. In this way, men have placed their identity in their job and have derived their primary self-esteem from it. Whenever a man's job is threatened he will become insecure, and whenever it is attacked he will become defensive. Men have come to live through their work and for their work. In a fast-changing world where work roles change quickly and there is no guarantee of long-term stability, men have become much more insecure. Too much of a man's sense of masculinity and self-identity has been tied up in whether he succeeds or fails in the world of work. This creates pressure on the man that may lead to any one of a number of stress reactions such as heart attacks, high blood pressure, ulcers, quick temper with family members, excessive drinking, long working hours, and moodiness.

On the other hand, women have traditionally attempted to define meaning and purpose in terms of their roles as wife and mother. Of the two, the motherhood role has been the one most used by women as the place where they centered their self-identity and self-esteem. In this way, women's identity becomes merely an extension of the achievements and failures of their children. When their children are happy they are happy; when their children hurt, they hurt. If their children are attacked, mothers tend to take it personally and attack back. The primary purpose of a woman's life from this perspective is to bear and raise children. At other times in a woman's life—before she has children, after she has raised children, or when she is unable to bear children—she places her primary identity in her role as a wife. When this happens, her self-esteem centers around her husband, his job, and the attention that he gives her. The woman begins to live through her husband's attention and job. Whenever primary meaning is derived from her role as a wife, a woman will gradually begin to try to bring happiness to her life through controlling and/or clinging to her husband. In most cases, this results in marriage problems.

As can be seen, none of these substitutes for true meaning outside of Christ can satisfy or bring happiness to one's life on a long-term basis because they have been cursed by God. This is discussed in Genesis 3:16-19. The curse upon woman was in terms of her role as mother—"I will greatly multiply thy sorrow in thy conception; in sorrow thou shalt bring forth children"—and her role as wife—"and thy desire shall be to thy husband and he shall rule over thee." Neither of these states reflect God's true plan and will, but stem from sin and the fall. Since the fall, women have tried to obtain too much of their self-identity and self-esteem from their roles as wife and mother. However, doing this only brings pain and suffering, as stated in Genesis. Eventually the children will grow up and the husband will give less attention to his wife. When this happens, the woman will again face her crisis of meaning—her life will seem meaningless.

The curse on man was on his work—"cursed is the ground for thy sake; in sorrow shalt thou eat of it all the days of thy life . . . . in the sweat of thy face shalt thou eat bread, till thou return unto the ground." The physical and psychological curse associated with work was not part of God's original plan, but came because of man's sin. For any man to place too much of his self-identity and self-esteem in his work role is a sin. The curse on work is that no matter how hard a man works, he will probably never get ahead and those few who do will eventually die. Every man who puts his primary meaning in his work role will eventually come to agree with the author of Ecclesiastes— "Vanity of vanity; all is vanity." It is probably because of this psychospiritual curse on work that men in this country have a shorter life span than women.

One thing that is certain about God's curses on man and woman is that we as human beings will not be able to overcome the curse through our own efforts. The solution is not to beat the curse, but to be released from it. However, to be released from the curse requires that we make Christ Lord of our life, something most people do not want to do. Many people in our churches today are struggling to find meaning and happiness through life roles when they could have true freedom in Christ.

Another attempt to overcome the curse is the modern-day women's liberation movement. The only problem with this movement is that it will never truly liberate women using its present philosophy. The women's lib movement is trying to free women from the curse on their roles as wife and mother by encouraging them to find meaning in work. As women transfer primary meaning from their mother/wife role to a work role, all they will get is a new form of slavery. Work will be just as cursed for women as it was for men if they try to derive from it their primary purpose and meaning in life.

One of the newer developmental phenomena being discussed today is the midlife crisis. This book will attempt to identify three adulthood stages, each with its own needs and crises. From this perspective we could talk about three adult life crises—one of meaning, one of relationship, and one of death. Each of these crises takes place at an appropriate time that can be considered normal. However, what most of those who have written about midlife crisis are referring to is not a normal part of the developmental sequence. The midlife crisis of meaning of the fallen man is merely a reassertion in middle adult life of the crisis of meaning that should have been resolved in the twenties. The reason it was not resolved was because during their twenties these people placed their primary identity in the roles that they were playing in life rather than in seeking God. The result is that in their forties and fifties the problem of the crisis of meaning returns as the roles of mother, wife, and worker begin to lose their ability to provide self-esteem and meaning.

This midlife crisis is pathological in that it is not inevitable and does not need to take place. Today, the trend in our fast-changing world seems to be that both men and women are experiencing the midlife crisis of meaning earlier and earlier. The roles that people play in life seem less and less to be able to block the problem of the underlying crisis of meaning that was never resolved.

Christians who do not understand that their primary meaning must come from God rather than roles can also experience a midlife crisis of meaning. We must help them see that if our identity is in Christ and our goal is to do the will of God, we should be able to change roles in life without being overwhelmed. When a woman can no longer be a mother, she needs to go to God and ask, "Now what do you want me to do? rather than get depressed. When a man's job is threatened or terminated, he should thank God for this opportunity to find a more effective way to serve Him. From God's perspective, the problem is not one of not enough jobs, but too few laborers. "The harvest truly is great, but the laborers are few, pray ye therefore the Lord of the harvest, that he would send forth laborers into his harvest" (Luke 10:2). It is only as we try to labor only for ourselves that we create psychological problems in terms of meaning and purpose for our lives. As we change the focus of our labors from self to others, there will no longer be a pathological midlife crisis of meaning. No matter where we go in life or how old we become, there will always be someone who needs God's message, God's love, and God's healing in his or her life.

BIBLICAL BASE

The Bible teaches us, therefore, that the Christian solution to the crisis of meaning in our lives is to place our identity in Christ as we seek to do the will of God. True independence and adult maturity come as we give up our plans for our life and begin to use God's blueprint. Life will yield more happiness and satisfaction as we live it God's way rather than self's way. This yielding begins with a commitment of our life to the Lordship of Christ. This brings us to the paradox of Christianity that the fallen man cannot and will not understand and/or accept. Adult Christianity is based on the idea that to become a free man we must become a slave to Christ by a choice of free will. If we try to remain free through choosing self over God, we will eventually become a slave to sin and to Satan. The paradox is that to get independence we must give it up and that if we refuse to give it up by holding onto it we will lose it.

The fallen man tries to reach independence through fulfilling his potential and only ends up frustrated because sin always undermines his efforts. The redeemed man seeks to reach independence through being restored to his potential by God. The fallen man approach is based on pride while the redeemed man approach is based on humility. As Christians, we must humbly affirm what John the Baptist said in John 3:30: "He must increase, but I must decrease." The Christian in Christ is a new man, as found in II Corinthians 5:17,18 where it says,

> If any man be in Christ he is a new creature: old things are passed away; behold all things become new. And all things are of God, who has reconciled us to himself by Jesus Christ, and given us the ministry of reconciliation.

An even stronger statement concerning finding meaning and identity through Jesus Christ is found in Galatians 2:20 as it states,

> I am crucified with Christ nevertheless I live; yet not I, but Christ liveth in me: and the life I now live in the flesh I live by the faith of the Son of God who loved me and gave himself for me.

This leads us to the strong statement of commitment to the cause of Christ made by Paul in Philippians 1:20,21, where he says,

> That in nothing I shall be ashamed, but that with all boldness, so now also Christ shall be magnified in my body, whether it be by life or by death. For me to live is Christ, and to die is gain.

Our commission in life as Christians is to fulfill the cause of Christ. Our worthiness to call ourselves Christians is directly related to how committed we are to this cause. Christ gives the charge to those who want to be his disciples in Matthew 28:18-20:

> All power is given unto me in heaven and earth Go ye therefore and teach (make disciples of) all nations, baptizing them in the name of the Father and of the Son and of the Holy Spirit: teaching them to observe all things whatsoever I have commanded you: and, lo, I am with you always even unto the end of the world.

Paul affirms this calling to spread the Gospel that Christ gave in II Corinthians 5:20 when he refers to Christians as "ambassadors for Christ." Our calling as Christians is to be ambassadors for Christ, spreading the good news of the Gospel message which is that there is true freedom of self in Christ—we can be set free from our bondage to Satan and sin.

The challenge to us is given by Paul in Ephesians 4:1, where he says, "I beseech you that you walk worthy of the vocation wherewith you are called." Jesus also challenges us in Matthew 5:14 and 16 when He states, "Ye are the light of the world . . . Let your light so shine before men that they may see your good works and glorify your father which is in heaven." To be a disciple of Christ, therefore, brings responsibility, but it also gives us a vision.

> Record the vision and inscribe it on tablets so that the one who reads may read it fluently. For the vision is yet for the appointed time; it hastens toward the goal, and it will not fail.
>
> *(Habakkuk 2:2,3)*

As Christians, we must obtain a vision for the world during the Meaning Stage and commit our life to it. Proverbs 29:18 indicates that, "where there is no vision the people perish." God promises in Acts 2:17 that:

> in the last days I will pour out my Spirit upon all flesh: and your sons and daughters shall prophesy and your young men shall see visions, and your old men shall dream dreams.
>
> *(cf. Joel 2:28)*

What we need today are more Christian young men and women who are willing to give up their dreams for self and get a vision of what their lives can do for God. Paul had a vision and remained true to it—"I was not disobedient unto the heavenly vision" (Acts 26:19). He stated the content of this vision in Acts 26:18, where he says God told him

> to open their eyes and to turn them from darkness to light, and from the power of Satan unto God, that they may receive forgiveness of sins and inheritance among them which are sanctified by faith that is in me.

May Paul's vision be the goal for all of us as Christians. The world is lost and people are doomed to hell; is there any one who still cares?

> Whosoever heareth these sayings of mine and doeth them I will liken unto a wise man which built his house upon a rock. And everyone that heareth these sayings of mine and doeth them not shall be likened unto a foolish man which built his house upon the sand . . . and it fell and great was the fall thereof.
>
> *(Matthew 5: 24,26,27)*

> Love not the world, neither the things that are in the world. If any man love the world the love of the Father is not in him. For all that is in the world, the lust of the flesh, the lust of the eye, and the pride of life, is not of the Father but is of the world. And the world passeth away and the lust there of, but he that doeth the will of God abideth forever.
>
> *(I John 2:15–17)*

HUMAN RESPONSIBILITY

As children reach the Meaning Stage, they are no longer children, whether they want to be or not. Childhood is over and adult responsibilities begin as we enter the twenties. In leaving childhood behind, young adults must choose to let go of parents as parents in terms of psychological dependence. On the other hand, parents must let go of their children as children in terms of continued control. From the young adult's perspective, there is a need to *break away* and stand alone in facing life's challenges and making life's decisions. This does not mean that the young adult can no longer seek counsel from his or her parents, only that the counsel is to be viewed as advice and not a decision. From the parent's perspective, there is a need to *let go* and give the child permission to be grownup. It is important for the parents to now respect the young adult's autonomy and trust in his or her judgment. In terms of psychological dynamics, the relationship needs to be changed from one between a parent and a child to one between an adult and an adult. Once young adults and parents can begin to relate to each other as adults, they will begin to develop a whole new relationship with each other. This new relationship will be one of equality, which also allows it to be one of friendship. The goal, therefore, is for the parent and child to reestablish their relationship as two adults where an adult friendship is able to develop based on respect and love.

Primary Responsibility

In terms of finding a meaning in life, the primary responsibility during the Meaning Stage is on the individual. Each young person as an adult now becomes responsible for his or her own choices and happiness. Being an independent adult means that there is now no one to blame other than self for life's problems. Self controls one's choices, and self creates one's future. Many people do not want to shoulder this burden of responsibility. They continue to blame their problems on others and refuse to take control of the decisions that will determine their future. This is a sign of immaturity and reflects that, although agewise the person is an adult, psychologically and spiritually he or she is still a child.

In the Bible becoming an adult is associated with free will and choice. Free will and choice eventually lead to responsibility and accountability. To become an adult, therefore, is to acknowledge one's free will and accept the responsibility for the choices that one makes.

To deny free will and responsibility is to remain a child. It makes no difference whether young adults accept free will or reject free will since as adults God still holds them accountable for their choices, even those made by default. The Meaning Stage between twenty and thirty years of age is a time where a person must gradually shift from focusing only on the privileges of independence to accepting the responsibilities of being an adult.

The young adult's search for meaning is a journey that must be traveled alone. There are no shortcuts and no one can find the answer for him or her. The search for meaning is a pilgrimage on which a person explores the possibilities of what he or she can do with his or her life. If the young adult cuts the journey short, it will reassert itself at some later point in life. In terms of psychospiritual development, not to find meaning during the Meaning Stage is to remain in childhood or in the Unstage. If a person fixates at this point, love and happiness will continually be searched for but never found. To place the primary responsibility for continued development on self during the Meaning Stage means that happiness can no longer be given or created by someone else; it must be found by self. No one else can make a person's life meaningful or give it purpose. From the Christian perspective, young adults need to turn away from parents and friends as sources of happiness and turn to God. God has a plan and purpose for every person's life that, when followed, will lead to fulfillment.

The secondary responsibility during the Meaning Stage is on adult society as a whole. Society has a vested interest in trying to help its young adults find a place in life where they can feel significant. If young adults can contribute to society as a whole, they will feel they are a part of the adult world. Society also has a vested interest in creating challenges and opportunities for its young adults. It is important that there continue to be new horizons to cross and new worlds to conquer. Finally, society has a vested interest in encouraging its young adults to have a vision of what they can do to make this place a better world in which to live. Young adults need to be able to dream about their future and feel like their lives will be important to the people around them.

Major Task

The major task of the Meaning Stage, then, is to encourage the young adult's quest for self-determination. All young adults heading into the adult world have feelings of uncertainty as to how they will do and whether they will make it. In terms of college students, this is especially relevant for graduating seniors. College, like childhood, is a sheltered environment that protects young adults from some of the harsh realities of the adult world. As a result, college students can continue to act irresponsibly and get away with it. When students leave college, just as when students who do not go to college leave high school, they must begin to face total accountability for their actions. Partly because of a lack of job opportunities and partly because we have not done a good job of raising our children, we have allowed adolescence to continue well into the twenties. Today there are many people in our society who at twenty-five still act like teenagers. Still, there is a point at which the immaturities and irresponsibilities will no longer be tolerated. Beyond that point, irresponsibility will bring unhappiness and social rejection.

Why is it that so many young adults act like children? Because they still feel emotionally as insecure as when they were children and because many times they are still treated like children. Society has a vested interest in overcoming its present trend toward permissiveness toward its young people. It needs to expect something from them, as well as demand something from them. The first demand that should be made is that young adults begin to act like young adults, not teenagers. The difference between the two is that the teenager focuses on freedom and the needs of self, while the mature young adult learns to focus more on responsibility and the needs of others. The task, then, is to convince the young adult that self-determination must be used for the good of society more than just for the good of self.

Major Technique

The major technique to be used to encourage young adults' quest for self-determination is to *give them a vision*. Challenge young adults with the potential that their lives can have an impact on society. This creates an immediate conflict over values. In a relativistic society, all values are equally good and all visions have equal worth. In reality, this is not true. There are many visions of glory or greatness that could be sought which have no social worth or value. Such visions as the desire to help those who are physically in need, the desire to be rich, the desire to be famous, the desire to be liked by others, the desire to produce a good product, and the desire to commit the perfect crime all do not have the same social value. Besides social value, these visions also do not have the same spiritual value. This means that it is possible to encourage the young adult in the direction of a vision that actually has very little social and/or spiritual value. From the Christian perspective, our desire is to give young people a vision that has eternal as well as temporal significance.

Focal Point

Giving young people a vision that has lasting social and spiritual value is only the first step. The second step is to *let them try it*. It is natural for young adults to be idealistic, to be dissatisfied with inequities and injustices within society. As young adults begin to see the reality of evil within the world, we encourage them to try to do something about it. We do our best to help them get a vision of what they can do to make this world a better place in which to live. A problem arises when young adults take the adult world seriously and set out to make changes. The usual response of society is to turn on young adults for trying to attack and undermine traditions. Now tradition by itself is not evil, but tradition for the sake of tradition is. This is true whether we are dealing with the factory, the government, or the church. Young adults become frustrated when they are told, on the one hand, to prove themselves, and then, on the other, not given a chance. We must find ways to channel the energy of young adults so that it can be used for the good of the society. If young adults are ignored or feel unneeded, they will begin to live for self. In reality most of the time we end up challenging the young adult to greatness while only seeking and rewarding mediocrity.

Goal of Stage

We have established in this section that young adults must become responsible for self as they seek to find meaning in life and society is responsible for encouraging the young adults' quest for self-determination by giving them a vision and then giving them the opportunity to try it. The goal is to help each young adult *to be able to find his or her unique purpose in life.* This is based on the Christian concept that when God created people He created them with a unique potential and a unique role to fill in the world. No two people are alike and God never uses the same life script twice. Every person is created by God with a specific place in God's plan for the world. In this way, every person is special to God as he or she fulfills the purpose for which God created him or her. Finding our purpose in life requires that we seek it through God's will for our life and not our own.

PSYCHOLOGICAL NEED

Basic Need

The basic need associated with the Meaning Stage is the need for *commitment*. Commitment must always be made to a cause. The cause in which we believe is tied to our vision or purpose in life. This means that the more young adults become committed to a particular cause, the more meaningful their lives will be. Young adults who do not become committed to some cause will eventually feel as if their lives are meaningless. Commitment to a cause brings meaning to life, but good causes are hard to find and even harder to hold onto. Since most people never make this kind of commitment, those who do are viewed as atypical and eventually are seen as a threat. To become committed to a cause is to become a radical, and radicals seek social and spiritual change in the lives of others. They seek to make converts to the cause and criticize those who do not join. The cause that most people become committed to is the *cause of mediocrity*. People who live for mediocrity do not like radicals coming into their world trying to make changes.

There is only one cause to which we can become committed that has eternal value, and that is the cause of Christ. For the Christian commitment to the cause centers around the Lordship of Christ in his or her life. One reason the church in our country has so little spiritual power is because there are too many people calling themselves Christians whose real commitment is to the cause of mediocrity rather than the cause of Christ. In conclusion, in our Christianity, without commitment to the cause of Christ there is no power and eventually no meaning.

The positive emotional state that comes through our commitment to the cause of Christ is *joy*. Joy is our response to our freedom in Christ and to a meaningful life that has a purpose. The more common word for joy being used today is happiness. The one thing that those people who live for the cause of mediocrity can never have is true joy and happiness. To put Christ in one's mind is not enough to bring joy to one's life; we must put Him on the throne seat of our heart. People can have many causes, including the cause of mediocrity, but the Bible teaches that the only cause that can bring joy and happiness is a commitment to the cause of Christ.

Psychological State

The psychological state associated with the Meaning Stage is *independence*. To be independent is to have a fully developed free will separate from the control and authority of parents. As discussed in the last chapter, it is possible to be an adult chronologically while still being a child in regard to one's psychospiritual development. From our discussion we found that the adaptive child adult was not independent because of a continued emotional dependence on others to make life's decisions. We also found that the rebellious child adult was not independent, because through rebellion toward authority he or she became enslaved by it. Rebellion was found to represent neither freedom nor independence. Finally, it was alluded to that the searching child adult in the wilderness has also not reached a state of independence. The searching child is still dependently bound to his or her need to search. True independence can only come in the Meaning Stage as the young adult gives up adaptation, rebellion, and searching and moves on to commitment. Independence comes as we use our free will to make a commitment to a cause. The only cause to which we can become committed in order to give our life lasting or eternal independence is the cause of Christ. This was reflected by Christ when He said, "And ye shall know the truth and the truth shall make you free" (John 8:32). Jesus also said in John 14:6, "I am the way, the truth, and the life: no man cometh unto the father, but by me."

Self-Esteem

Primary self-esteem during the Meaning Stage is derived from meeting our need for commitment. *The value of self is determined by the value of the cause in which we believe.* If we choose a cause that has meaning, our life will have meaning; the depth or superficiality of the cause will determine the depth or superficiality of our life. If we do not have a cause, we remain fixated in the Unstage or wilderness of life, drifting with no apparent purpose or direction. If our cause is shallow or superficial, our life will be viewed by self as shallow or superficial. If we become committed to the cause of mediocrity, our life will be mediocre. If our cause is based on temporal value, our life will have no eternal purpose. From the Christian perspective, our goal is to become committed to the cause of Christ through choosing the Lordship of Christ in our life. There is no virtue in the eyes of God in being lukewarm or mediocre; as Christians we should all strive for the cause of greatness for God as we share the Gospel of Christ with the world. Every Christian needs to make their belief in God something that has substance. It is time that we stand up boldly and be the salt of the earth and light of the world that God wants us to be.

As in childhood, sin is still an ever-present reality in the life of adults. Even those who are Christians still have a sin nature that can affect their life and lead to sin. In the life of the young adult during the Meaning Stage, sin is still inevitable and psychospiritual health is not immediate or automatic. As a result, every young adult will experience the reality of sin and the fall as it relates to the Meaning Stage and will have to face and overcome the negative aspects of this stage before progressing to the next. This means that positive psychospiritual growth through the three adult stages will be marked by three cycles of fall and rise.

The steps of the cycle are threefold. The person first seeks a human psychological resolution to the stage; second, human attempts at controlling the process will fail and development will be marred; and third, the person can turn to God for a spiritual solution to the life crisis through a reconfirmation of the Lordship of Christ.

Negative Cognitive State

The cognitive state that is experienced when a person is unable to find lasting purpose or direction in life is the state of *meaninglessness*. Either life has meaning or it becomes meaningless. As discussed at the beginning of this chapter, every young adult comes to a point in the developmental process at which there arises a *crisis of meaning*. The human psychological solution to this problem is to find meaning in roles. The male tends to look for meaning in his work role, while the woman has traditionally attempted to find meaning in her roles as wife and mother, although many women are also seeking meaning in work roles. But the psychospiritual task of finding meaning in life cannot be truly fulfilled only through life's roles. As a result, sometime later in every person's life the crisis of meaning will reassert itself. When the human psychological solution has failed, people will begin to experience psychological conflict.

Two negative emotional states are associated with the crisis of meaning, whether it is occurring for the first time in the young adult or reoccurring for a second time in middle adult life. The first negative emotional state associated with the crisis of meaning is *depression*. The first reaction many people have when they begin to sense that their life is meaningless and futile is one of being depressed. People who are depressed are miserable; they have no joy, life no longer seems fun, and responsibilities seem too hard to bear. The central element in those people who react to the lack of meaning in life by becoming depressed is that there is a strong sense of self-guilt and blame—"My life is meaningless and its my fault." Those who become depressed also have an underlying problem with self-worth or value—"My life is meaningless because I am worthless." These people take a passive approach to finding meaning as they consider themselves pawns in the hands of fate—"My life is meaningless and there is nothing I can do about it."

The second negative emotional reaction to the problem of meaninglessness is *bitterness*. The person who becomes depressed blames themselves for the problem of lack of meaning; the person who becomes bitter blames others. The bitter person also experiences a lack of joy and happiness when life does turn out the way he or she wants and takes out his or her frustration on others. The bitter person blames God for the lack of blessings. The real problem behind bitterness is not that others failed the person, but that the person failed him or herself. Since meaning in life cannot be given to a person by others, it cannot be kept from him or her by others. Bitterness is almost always found in people who are very selfish and self-centered. Bitter people want to get too much and give too little.

Primary Fear

The primary fear stemming from our search for meaning is represented by the words *I am lost*. The young adult heading into the adult world is entering scary territory with no clear roadmap of where to go. Questions concerning schooling, career, and marriage are central to the direction in which one heads and the nature of the journey. The problem is that there are no guarantees. Millions of people find themselves lost in their marriage, as reflected in the rising divorce rate. Millions of others are feeling lost as to vocational adjustment and career development. The women's liberation movement has produced millions of women who feel lost as to what their role in society should be in their search for meaning. This sense of being lost can only be overcome by finding a cause to which one can become committed. Unfortunately, many of these people who are lost will be led into causes that are destructive. There are many people in the world who prey on lost people, leading them astray into causes that only serve the selfish purposes of the leader.

Existential Sin

The existential sin associated with the Meaning Stgae is that of *idolatry*. In our Exodus analogy the biggest danger to be confronted in the Promised Land is the lure of false idols or gods. For the young adult, the same problem is true. Idolatry is the elevation of some thing, person, or goal to the status of a god. This problem of idolatry associated with the Meaning State is discussed in the Bible in terms of the word *treasures*.

> Lay not up for yourselves treasures on earth where moth and rust doth corrupt and where thieves break through and steal: but lay up for yourselves treasures in heaven, where neither moth nor rust doth corrupt and where thieves do not break through and steal: for where your treasure is, there will your heart be also.
>
> *(Matthew 6:19–21)*

The point here is that we attempt to derive meaning from where we seek our treasure. The seeking of treasures reflects the true cause to which we are committed. The Bible indicates that the treasures of earth are only temporary and cannot give life-lasting meaning. The earthly treasures of life become our *idols*. Idolatry as a sin, then, is a part of every person's life from young adulthood throughout the rest of life. The neurotic fantasy associated with idolatry is *I can find happiness in the fulfillment of only my needs*. The difference between treasures on earth and treasures in heaven is that the former is determined by what we do for self, the latter is determined by what we do for others.

MEANING STAGE

Human Responsibility

Primary Responsibility	**Self**
Major Task	To encourage the young adult's quest for self-determination.
Technique	**Give them a vision.**
Focal Point	**Let them try it.**
Goal	To be able to find my **unique** purpose in life.

Psychological Need

Basic Need	**Commitment**
Resultant Positive Emotion	**Joy**
Psychological State	**Independence**
Self-Esteem	I am the **cause** in which I believe.

Human Fall

Negative Cognitive State	**Meaninglessness**
Resultant Negative Emotions	**Depression Bitterness**
Primary Fear	**I am lost.**
Existential Sin	**Idolatry**
Neurotic Fantasy	I can find happiness through the fulfillment of only my needs.

10
Love Stage

The Love Stage runs from approximately ages twenty-five to forty-five and corresponds with the Biblical Era associated with the Holy Spirit. This period is also sometimes called the Church Age, and it is the one which we are in now. Adulthood is reached during the identity stage, when a person becomes independently responsible for what he or she does and what he or she becomes as an individual. But a person cannot stop there because humans were created in such a way that to be complete or whole we must be in relationship. We are social beings and, therefore, are left unfulfilled if we are without close social relationships. Everyone wants to have friends. Everyone wants to be loved. This is the task of the Love Stage—to learn how to relate in a meaningful way.

Independence is not the end of a person's adult psychospiritual development, but merely the first step. We progress from a state of dependency as a child to a state of independency as a young adult to a state of interdependency as a more mature adult. A person in a state of dependency says, "I need you to help me." A person in a state of independency says, "I do not need any help, I can do it myself." A person in a state of interdependency says, "I need your help and you need mine; let us do it together."

In the field of psychology too much emphasis has been placed on the concepts of freedom, autonomy, and independence. What is not always acknolwedged is our need to relate; to love and be loved. The issue in the Love Stage, then, is one of learning how to love. This is a task that we spend most of the rest of our adult lives trying to master. The reality is that few ever learn the true meaning of love and become capable of being loving persons. One reason for this is that few people ever learn the true source of love.

Love is one of the most used terms in the English vocabulary but probably the least understood. One would lose track trying to compile all the songs, poems, movies, plays, and stories ever written about love. In our society today, love is most often defined in terms of romance and sex, whether it be heterosexual or homosexual. Two people have sexual intercourse hoping to find love and then become disillusioned when all they find is increased loneliness as they treat each other as objects of self-gratification. Romance and love are also two different things. Romance is an illusion based on a fantasy of what we want someone to be. As a fantasy, it is a bubble waiting to be popped when the illusion is destroyed, as it inevitably will be. Why are so many looking for love and yet so few finding it? Because they have an inadequate definition of love.

BIBLICAL BASE

The Bible teaches us that all human definitions of love will be inadequate because of an inadequate measuring rod or standard. There is only one standard by which we are to judge as to whether something is love or not, and that is God Himself. It is stated in I John 4:8 that "God is love." The measure of this love is found in verse 10, where it says, "herein is love, not that we loved God, but that He loved us, and sent His Son to be the propitiation for our sins." John 3:16 tells us that "God so loved the world that He gave His only begotten Son, that

whosoever believeth in Him should not perish, but have eternal life."
God by His very nature is love, and since we are the creature, not the
creator, any love that we have or give must come from God, the source.
This truth is stated in I John 4:7,8, where it says that "love is of God;
and every one that loves is born of God and knows God. He that loves
not knows not God." This Scripture gives two truths. The first truth is
that no human being is truly capable of loving unless he or she knows
God. The second truth is that even those who know God are unable to
love except that love is given to them by God through His Holy Spirit.
This is confirmed in I John 4:16, which states that, "God is love and
he that dwells in love dwells in God and God in him." As Christians,
we become the sons of God, able to love as God does. Galatians 4:6
says, "and because you are sons, God has sent forth the Spirit of His
Son into your hearts."

The result of defining love in terms of God is that the standard
becomes real as well as absolute. As long as we continue to define love
from a human perspective, love remains abstract and relative. It is a
fantasy to think that each one of us can create our own private definition of love and through it obtain personal happiness. The ultimate
irony of man trying to play God is that he only succeeds in destroying
himself. In terms of our discussion of love, the personal definitions that
we create in rebellion against God's definition only lead to frustration
and disillusionment when the sex and romance that was called love dis-
integrates into heartache and bitterness. If we turn to God as our source
of love, He will give it to us through the Holy Spirit. As we are able to
love and be loved, we are able to be intimate with God, with ourself,
and with others. This is the interdependency that was mentioned and is
represented in the passage in John 13:35, which says, "By this shall all
men know that you are my disciples, if you have love one to another."
It is also found in I Corinthians 12:12,13, where it states, "For as the
body is one and has many members, and all the members of that one
body, being many, are one body: so also, is Christ. For by one Spirit
are we all baptized into one body." The principle that this passage goes
on to develop is that as Christians we need each other. As we express

our needs to each other we experience intimacy. As we help each other to meet those needs, we express love.

One of the misconceptions that many Christians have which holds back their spiritual growth is that they must be careful that they do not love themselves too much. The definitional problem here is that love is being equated with conceit, not with God. If a Christian were asked whether it would be possible to love God too much, he or she would quickly answer no. However, when Christians are asked if it is possible to love themselves too much, most would answer yes. They do not realize that they have allowed themselves to change their definition of love. If love is real and absolute, it is the same love whether we love God, ourselves, or our neighbor. This is consistent with Scriptural teaching, which tells us in Matthew 22:39 that, "Thou shalt love thy neighbor as you love yourself." Christians need to see that it is impossible to love themselves too much. The conceited person is not one who loves himself too much, but one who loves himself too little. A person's conceit is nothing more than a façade covering that person's true feelings of inadequacy and inferiority.

Actually our ability to love God and to love our neighbor is limited by our ability to love ourselves. We cannot love God more than we love our neighbor and we cannot love our neighbor more than we love ourselves. What we discover is that love is a circle that begins with God, since He is the source of love. Out of His love for us He sent His Son to die to overcome the separation between man and God because of man's sin. Through this sacrifice we can see God's love for us and, as a result, learn to accept and love ourselves. When we begin to love ourselves, we experience the joy and excitement of our salvation and we become motivated to show and tell others about this love. In this way, we begin to love our neighbor. In the Bible, God tells us that we love Him through the love we show to our neighbor, so the circle is completed as the love God gave to us through the Holy Spirit is returned to Him as we allow it to flow through us to the people around us. Through this discussion we can now define love as *a commitment to a relationship involving our whole personality where we attempt to meet the true needs of the one being loved through the leading and power of the Spirit of God.*

HUMAN RESPONSIBILITY

Primary Responsibility

The primary responsbility for human relationship rests upon all adults. God created man as a social being with a need to relate and the responsibility to meet this need must be shared by everyone. The world in which we live will not be a caring place unless individuals are willing to care. Caring for others is in contrast to its opposite, which is caring for self. The main enemy of love is egocentrism or selfishness. The more selfish we are, the less we care about others. We have not adequately understood that egocentrism is a self-defeating strategy. As an adult, one cannot find long-term meaning in life while at the same time choosing to ignore the feelings and needs of others. If we ignore the need of others for intimacy and love, we also ignore the same need in self. Today millions of adults want to be loved, but, because of their egocentrism, refuse to give love. Since love is something that must be shared, it is impossible to have love when people only want to take from a relationship but resist making any commitment to give in return.

This means that in the Love Stage another commitment needs to be made. Where, in the Meaning Stage, our commitment is to the cause of finding life's calling, in the Love Stage the commitment must be to other people. In reality, the two commitments ultimately cannot be separated. Finding a life's calling that has lasting value eventually must include the element of social responsibility. As adults we are linked together in a social context so that what one does affects all. To the extent that the needs of some people in a society are neglected, eventually everyone will suffer. This is why we need to have a social conscience; it is in our own best interest. It is also why we need to fight against prejudice, discrimination, and social injustice. All adults need to see every other person as a human brother or sister worthy of our love.

In terms of the church, we refer to the corporate unit as the Body of Christ. In the larger social context, we must also see ourselves as part of the brotherhood of man. There is no person living who was not created by God, who is not loved by God, and for whom Christ's atonement is not available. There is no person living to whom we should not be willing to reach out a hand of love or with whom we should not share the Gospel message. Too many so-called Christians and Christian churches misrepresent true Christianity by focusing more on the size of the congregation, the size of the building, the size of the offering, and the church program than they do on the true needs of the people in the community around them. Many so-called Christians spend more time fighting among themselves than they do loving each other and the people of the world. It is no wonder that so many people reject this brand of self-centered, self-righteous Christianity. This is not Christianity. God's message for us today is a message of love to man. If we do not reflect God's love and share God's love, we really are not being a Christian.

Major Task

The major task of the Love Stage is that we establish relationships with others on the basis of equal spiritual worth. During childhood, the evaluation of people often was made on the basis of that which makes them unequal. As discussed in the Behavior Stage, three of these variables that are judged to be important in children are intelligence, athletic abilities, and beauty. This same process continues in our adult life with new symbols such as money, social status, and political power. In this way, first as children and then as adults, we are divided into the haves and the have-nots. Most of our social relationships are structured on this basis when we socialize only with those who are at our level of social value. This process of establishing restricted social relationships on the basis of shared inequality is called making friends. But this is not true friendship; this is not true love. True love and friendship do not shut people out because of their social status or apparent lack of social worth. The Bible teaches that these social differences that we use to judge people and establish our friendships are merely temporal distinctions. On the other hand, God does not judge on the basis of what we are on the outside, but of what we are on the inside. If we reserve our love and friendships only for those who we perceive as socially desirable, we do not have God's true love and this is not real friendship. Friendship comes when we relate to people as people as we acknowledge that in the eyes of God we are all of equal value.

Technique

To establish adult friendships with people requires involvement, and involvement takes time. The primary technique that we use to love, then, is to *spend time with*. It is impossible to love people if we do not know them. We cannot get to know them until we spend time with them. There cannot be love without some kind of involvement. There cannot be friendship without social interaction. The problem comes, however, in that so much of our social involvement and interaction are still basically egocentric. Most of our talk centers around us, and most of our attention is focused on our needs. For the natural man, it is easy to talk about self, but hard to listen to others. The natural man also finds it easy to notice the needs of self, but hard to notice the needs of others. To love, then, requires not only that we get involved in the lives of others, but that we also begin to learn how to focus more on their needs than we do on our own.

Focal Point

The key word for the Love Stage as we seek to establish friendships is *communication*. The primary need of the Love Stage for adults is intimacy, and true intimacy can only come through communication. The focal point for communication can be summed up in the words *open up*. For communication to lead to friendship and intimacy, people must begin to share what they really think and feel—about life and about each other. Every person has thoughts, feelings, and motives within self for which he or she is ashamed and does not want others to know for fear of being rejected or judged. Every person also has thoughts, feelings, and motives which, if shared, would make him or her vulnerable to hurt. As a result, from adolescence, when we first discover our inner self as well as our own vulnerability to hurt and criticism, we begin to close our true self off from people. We become afraid to let people know what we really think and feel. Instead, we create a social mask that we wear, showing only those parts of self that we think people will like. We have created a façade, a false front, behind which we hide as we try to protect self from attack. In doing this, we separate what we are on the outside from what we are on the inside.

In the end we all feel like phonies, going through life playing a game—fooling people but afraid to be ourselves. To the extent that we hide behind this mask or façade, we are inauthentic. We are lying to the world; we are lying to ourselves; and we are lying to God. To become authentic, real, and whole again we must be honest with ourselves. We must look behind the mask and see what we are really like. We need to work on those aspects of self that we do not like. Second, we need to be honest with God. In reality, we cannot hide anything from God; we only think we can. God knows what we have done and what we think and feel before we tell Him. Being honest with God is not something we do to inform God but so that God can heal us and make us whole again. Finally, we need to be honest with others. This is what we mean by opening up. We must open up to self, to God, and to others. In doing this, we allow God's love to permeate inside our shells and change us so that we can love ourselves and love others. It is impossible to love, to experience intimacy, and to have friendships in an authentic way until we open up.

Goal of Stage

The goal of the Love Stage is that we be able to come to a point in our life where we are *able to give and receive love*. True love is never a one-sided relationship. To define love in terms of taking or getting is not true love, since we also need to learn how to give. To define love only in terms of giving or sharing is also not true love, since we also need to receive. True love and friendship involves a reciprocal relationship in which all are free to give and receive. To take love without being willing to share love reflects greed and selfishness. On the other hand, to give love to those in need without being willing to receive from them in return reflects piety and spiritual superiority.

Today we too often have allowed one-sided concepts of human relationships to be called love. In a dating relationship, for example, a girl might define how much she loves a boy on the basis of how much she needs him. This is not really love since the focus is primarily only on self. On the other hand, a church member might define love on the basis of giving a poor family food at Christmas. In this example, the church member feels good because of his or her charity, while the poor person's self-esteem is undermined. A much higher expression of love would be to give the father of the poor family a job and allow him to work for his food. Through this approach, both are able to give and receive. As a society, we have come to redefine social love as social charity where the government takes from those who do not want to give and gives to those in need of something they do not want. In doing this, we are destroying the social conscience of the former and the social dignity of the latter. Both groups become angry and frustrated. We need to use government less and our social conscience more to deal with the problems of prejudice, discrimination, and social injustice. In this way, we will have much more love in our world.

PSYCHOLOGICAL NEED

Basic Need

The primary need that we experience in relation to the Love Stage is *intimacy*. Intimacy can be defined as *the involvement of two or more people in an interdependent relationship of love based upon a shared perception of spiritual equality and human value.* Through intimacy, we can develop the ability to be sensitive to the needs and feelings of others. The resultant positive emotion that stems from true intimacy in our adult relationships is *compassion*. Compassion for other people comes as we are able to see their lives from their perspective. In doing this, we can empathize with their sorrows and share in their blessings. It is impossible to have compassion for other people without involvement and communication. This means that compassion becomes a byproduct of our social intimacy with others and not the cause of it. Without intimate relationships as adults, we cannot find the love that we all seek. For many people, usually male, the desire for love and intimacy are seen as signs of weakness, especially in the early years of adulthood. One of the signs of developing maturity during middle adulthood is when these people begin to see the importance and value of intimacy to their own psychospiritual development. The need is to discover the importance of positive relationships with other people to our own psychological health.

One problem that Christians, as well as non-Christians, have is one of not being able to distinguish between acceptance and intimacy. Acceptance relates to our need to be liked, stemming from the Motive Stage of development, and is that which we experience when we are accepted and liked by others on the basis of social conformity. Earlier in this chapter, it was suggested that true love and intimacy are rare in interpersonal relationships between people. What we find is that most people, because they do not know how to discover true love and intimacy, choose acceptance as a cheap substitute. It is a sad fact, but true, that even many of the people who are associated with our churches have never really experienced true intimacy and love within that church setting.

There are four different types of relationships in which the goal is intimacy. The first is the friendship that we have with people in general; the second is the relationship that exists between a husband and wife in marriage; the third is the special fellowship that we can have with each other as Christians; and the fourth is the personal relationship that we can have with God. As adults, all of these relationships can be based on either a concept of acceptance or a concept of intimacy.

If we are oriented toward acceptance in our friendships, conformity will be the central issue; in our marriage, the roles and duties of the husband and wife are primary; in the church, we are most concerned about membership; and with God, the issue is complying with His laws. If we are oriented toward intimacy, acceptance of diversity will mark our friendships; communication will be considered most important in husband and wife relationships; fellowship will be more important than membership as it relates to our view of church; and an inward personal relationship with God will be more important than an outward conformity to His laws. Acceptance is the web within which adolescents get trapped by the extreme conformity demanded by the peer group as the price for being liked. What most adults do not realize is that they are just as trapped as the adolescent in their need to be accepted and liked by others. When adults continue to seek fulfilling relationships only through acceptance, they are condemning themselves to an emptiness that can only be filled through true intimacy. The following chart represents what we have been discussing.

	Acceptance	Intimacy
FRIENDSHIPS	Unity in Conformity	Unity in Diversity
MARRIAGE	Focus on roles and duties (50/50)	Focus on communication (100/100)
CHURCH	Membership (Size)	Fellowship (Quality)
GOD	God as parent	God as friend
	Talk at God	Talk with God
	Doing for God	Becoming for God

Psychological State

We have now established that in the Love Stage of life the primary need is intimacy. Intimacy was defined as two people in a relationship where they are both able to give and receive love. The psychological state that these people are in when they are able to be intimate and share love is the state of interdependency. There is a difference between the state of dependency, where one adult leans on another adult and needs another adult, and interdependency, which is based on compassion and not need. It is understandable that children are emotionally dependent since, as children, that is all they can be. However, adults are capable of more in their adult relationships than just more childhood dependency in adult forms.

For example, in a marriage, we seem to assume that just because two people get married they must love each other. In reality, people do not get married because of love but in order to learn how to love. To have love in a marriage requires that the couple have intimacy and to have intimacy the two people must psychologically and spiritually grow up and quit being children. Most couples getting married today are doing so while still in states of emotional dependency, which means the marriage is based on neurotic need and not love. To have love and intimacy in a marriage requires that both people first must become adults.

To become an adult requires that we first go through the Unstage and the Meaning Stage. One does not get to love just by becoming twenty-five. One gets to the Love Stage by completing the stages that come before it. This is why, agewise, the beginning of the Love Stage was placed much later than when most people in our society think they find true love. What we are saying is that, in terms of this theory, love develops much later as a force in our lives than we have thought and it takes much longer to learn how to do it successfully than we had anticipated. This means that what people have been calling love is not love, but an illusion of love. This also means that finding and sharing love are not easy things to do. Today the reality of a high divorce rate reflects that the illusions of love used by people to build their marriages are not working. We need to begin to encourage people to start looking for real love and not some cheap substitute.

In the same way that people misinterpret the meaning of love in marriage, they also misinterpret it in adult friendships. Being liked by others by doing that which will please them is not love. Doing for others what they need to learn to do for themselves is not love. True love in human relationships encourages people to fulfill the potential that God has for them by pleasing God, not pleasing us. Too many adults, even in Christian circles, define love only on the basis of what people do to us or for us. Since love comes from God, true love can only be based upon what we do in the power of God that is positive to others and for others. In other words, today the primary focus in our concept of love has been shifted from the needs of others to the needs of self.

By defining the Love Stage as involving a psychological state of interdependency, we are limiting the capacity and ability to love only to adults. This might seem rather extreme, but what we are saying is that only adults can love as an act or choice of free will. Children can love only as a response to being loved, and the love can only be one-sided. This also means that children are incapable of being involved in and experiencing true intimacy because of maturational limitations. True intimacy cannot take place between a child and a child, or between a parent and a child. This is true both in terms of chronological age maturity and psychological age maturity. Neither the person who is agewise a child nor the person who is emotionally a child is capable of experiencing true intimacy and love in their human relationships. True intimacy, then, can only be experienced by an adult with an adult when they are acting like adults. This means that children can have true love and intimacy in their relationships with their parents, but they cannot do it until they grow up. A parent-child relationship by itself is not love, but merely creates the potential for love. This potential, however, cannot be fulfilled until the parent and child become each other's friends as adults. The same is true for siblings. For siblings to have true love and intimacy for each other, they must reestablish their relationship after they grow up. Otherwise, the emotional ties that hold them together are merely memories.

Self-Esteem

There can be no real love and no real intimacy in our lives as adults unless we choose to invest some of our psychic energy and some of our time in trying to establish good relationships with people. As in most of the stages, the primary enemy is egocentrism. Egocentrism, as it relates to love, means that the more we get wrapped up in ourselves, in terms of our needs and our goals in life, the less time we will invest in the lives of others. Egocentrism leads to a view of society and life based on competition with others. This means that in order for me to get ahead in life I must compete with and beat others. In the Behavior Stage, we pointed out that this is not true. Our real competition in life is not with others, but with ourselves. The goal is not to be the best, but only to do our best. If we are trying to be the best as adults, people either become enemies that need to be attacked or suckers to be used. If we are trying to do our best, people become friends to help us along the way. The focus here is on cooperation and helping each other. We now are free to give and share as well as take. If we underestimate the importance of people to being a success and leading a fulfilled life, we will create a crisis of relationship in middle adulthood.

This midlife crisis of relationship is different from the midlife crisis of meaning, although the two overlap. If, in our attempts to find meaning in life, we do not include the importance of people to our own psychospiritual health, eventually we will create conflict in our lives. The crisis of relationship usually comes in the late thirties or early forties when a person finds that living only for self is empty. A father who has neglected his children throughout much of their childhood because he was driven to achieve success in his career suddenly finds his career development stale or empty and has a desire to get to know his children better. The problem, however, is that many times the children no longer want to get to know their father and a crisis of relationship is created in the father. As a result, he experiences guilt over the fact that he did not spend more time being a father when he had the opportunity.

Our self-esteem, then, during the Love Stage is built from the experiences of closeness that we have in our human relationships. We all have a need for closeness, and *closeness results when we are being authentic in human relationships*. The problem stems from the fact that just being close to people by itself does not create self-esteem. Because of the sinful nature in all of us, there is no guarantee that our experiences of closeness with others will be positive. Through closeness, we can hurt just as easily as we can love. The goal for the Christian, then, is not just to be close, but that God's Holy Spirit and love will permeate us as we are close to people so that their lives will be changed for the better. Closeness controlled by God's Holy Spirit heals lives. Closeness controlled by self or Satan destroys lives. As Christians, we can evaluate how much real love we have by looking at the lives of the people with which we come in contact. We must ask the question as to whether we are a *stepping stone* or a *stumbling block* in the lives of the people with whom we are close. As we do this, we begin to understand the next stage, which has to do with fruit. In God's eyes, our fruit will be people and what our life has done to and for people. This is the only treasure that we will carry into eternity. Self-esteem, then, in the Love Stage can only be built through the positive affect that our life has on the lives of others.

HUMAN FALL

Again, as in all of the previous stages, the fall is inevitable and universal. Every person, including every Christian, will need to face their crisis of relationship eventually. This crisis of relationship comes when we are able to see that as humans we do not have the capacity to love and that without God our need for love will never be met. It is only when our feeble attempts at finding love and intimacy have failed that we will turn to God and seek to let Him control our marriages, our families, and our friendships. Since we usually do not do this without first struggling with self, we all must go through the psychological and spiritual conflict of the fall as it relates to the Love Stage.

Negative Cognitive State

At the point in our life where we experience the crisis of relationship, we find ourselves in the cognitive state of *aloneness*. The opposite of intimacy and love is to be existentially alone. To not be close to others is to be separate from others. There are many ways of being separate where we try to deny or ignore our aloneness. However, it is just a matter of time until these techniques of defense against aloneness will fail and we will experience a crisis of relationship.

God did not create man to be alone. The reason given by God for the creation of Eve was that Adam was not meant to be alone. By our very spiritual nature, we must have relationship, we must have love. Aloneness first was experienced by Adam and Eve in the Garden. It came through sin when they found themselves cut off from God's fellowship and love. This means that at root the state of aloneness is not a social problem, but a spiritual problem. We will not be able to overcome the negative cognitive state of aloneness in our human relationships until we have restored ourselves with God, our Creator. We will not be able to have true fellowship and intimacy with others until we first have fellowship with God. This means that before we try to make people our friends, whether parent, spouse, or buddy, we need to make God our friend. Not only does God need to be our friend, He needs to become our best friend. If we try to make people rather than God our source of love, we will eventually find ourselves alone. People's love will fail us, but God's love never fails.

There are two negative emotional states that stem from the state of aloneness. The first of these is *despair*. Despair comes into our lives when we find ourselves alone and feeling like nobody cares. Everyone that we looked to for love and comfort has failed us. The person in an emotional state of despair feels as if he or she is in a dark tunnel. They see no light at the end, they feel lost, they feel like the world is closing in on them, and they feel alone. This aloneness is different than the loneliness experienced during adolescence. Teenagers feel that love is possible and that the only problem is that they just have not found it yet. The person in the cognitive state of aloneness experiencing the emotion of despair feels that love is hopeless. Despair stems from the view that I am not loved and will not ever be loved because for me love is not to be found. For the person in a state of despair, the reason for this inability to find love is that "I am unloveable." This warped thinking is based on the idea that, since no one loves me, I must be worthless. Once a person reaches this step in his or her thinking, it is just a matter of time until he or she begins to have suicidal thoughts. Suicide must be seen as more than a psychological problem since at root the cause is spiritual. People who are having suicidal thoughts are actually involved in spiritual warfare with Satan and they need our help. Help comes, however, not as we give them our love, but as we give them God's love.

The second negative emotional state associated with the cognitive state of aloneness is that of *indifference*. The second major reaction that we can have when we discover that there is no love in our life is to rebel. In this way, we find that it is the adaptive child state that reacts to aloneness with despair, while it is the rebellious child state that reacts to aloneness with indifference. The final way of expressing our hostility to society, to authority, to people, to parents, and to life is to become indifferent. This indifference of the Love Stage stems out of the bitterness of the Meaning Stage. First we become bitter, then we become indifferent. Since the indifferent person does not care about being loved by people, he or she can turn people into objects of manipulation. People are used for the person's own selfish purposes and then are discarded with no sense of guilt or remorse. The philosophy of the indifferent person is that life is a con, so you better get people before they get you.

Primary Fear

The primary fear associated with the fall is the idea that *nobody cares*. The people experiencing the emotion of despair feel like nobody cares and if nobody cares then they are lost and life is hopeless. On the other hand, people experiencing the emotion of indifference feel that since nobody else cares, why should they care either. Both groups of people are in a state of aloneness and both are angry at others and the world because they feel neglected and rejected. People in despair channel their anger into an attack on themselves through depression and/or suicide. Through this cry of despair, it is hoped that someone will hear them and care. People in indifference channel their anger into an attack on others and society for being hypocritical—promising to care, promising to love, but always breaking their promises. Both types of people have the attitude of "What's the use?" and do not trust others anymore. They view most of the attempts by do-gooders at offering a hand as merely words, lies, and cons. The idea that nobody cares eventually leads to skepticism and cynicism.

Existential Sin

The existential sin that results when we give up on our attempts to establish love and intimacy in our human relationships is that we *quench the Holy Spirit*. The Holy Spirit of God seeks to work within us to show us our need for love and offers to fill this need through Jesus Christ. Even in our lives as Christians the Holy Spirit daily seeks to teach us more about how to love, as well as how much God loves us. If

---

LOVE STAGE

Human Responsibility

Primary Responsibility	**Adults as friends**
Major Task	To establish friendships on the basis of equal spiritual worth.
Technique	**Spend time with**
Focal Point	**Open self up**
Goal	To be able to give and receive love.

Psychological Need

Basic Need	**Intimacy**
Resultant Positive Emotion	**Compassion**
Psychological State	**Interdependency**
Self-Esteem	I am **close** when I am being authentic in relationships.

Human Fall

Aloneness
↓   ↓

Negative Cognitive State	
Resultant Negative Emotions	**Despair Indifference**
Primary Fear	**Nobody cares**
Existential Sin	**Quench the Holy Spirit**
Neurotic Fantasy	I do not need God's love.

---

we block this working of the Holy Spirit in our lives, we commit the sin of quenching the Holy Spirit. The primary purpose of the Holy Spirit, then, is to meet our need for love and to show us how to love. If we seek love from others before we seek love from God, we commit sin. This truth is represented in Matthew 22:37, where Jesus said, "Thou shalt love the Lord thy God with all thy heart, and with all thy soul, and with all thy mind." To love God was given as the first and greatest commandment. The problem comes when we try to love God and love people before we allow God's love to permeate and change us. It is impossible for someone who feels unloved and unloveable to love anyone. In other words, in order to love we must first be loved, and the primary source of this love is God. The neurotic fantasy that accompanies the sin of quenching the Holy Spirit is that *I do not need God or His love to experience love in my life*. In reality, God is love, and true love only comes from God.

11
Fruit Stage

The final stage in the developmental sequence is the Fruit Stage. It begins in middle adulthood, usually after age forty, and continues until we die. The Fruit Stage corresponds with the Biblical Era that is to come in terms of God the Father and eternal life. In this way, fruit has both a temporal, social reality, and an eternal, spiritual reality. This means that the fruit of our life will not only be evaluated by people and society, it will also be evaluated by God. In the end, God's judgment of our lives will be the decisive one, since it will determine our eternal fate—whether for eternity we will have spiritual life or spiritual death. This same judgment will determine whether for eternity we will exist in heaven or in hell. The Christian who believes in God and His Word, as recorded in the Bible, must acknowledge that the Bible teaches a final judgment that will include all people. Adults will have their lives judged by their fruit and God will be the one to decide whether the fruit was good or evil.

The goal of the Fruit Stage is to accomplish and create something of value through one's efforts that will be a positive contribution to the world in which we live. All people have a desire to do something during their lifetime that will generate themselves out beyond that life—

that will leave its mark on the community and people around them. All of us want to be famous so that we will be remembered after we die, even if it's only by one person. The basic need of each of us is that the efforts and struggles that we must cope with as adults should have some significance. If the efforts of our lives have true value in that they meet the true needs of people, we move on from the state of interdependence to the state of transcendence. In this way, life continues to generate itself out into the future—each generation building upon the one before it. Also, the Fruit Stage overlaps with the Love Stage. This means that as adults we have two concerns that are important to our psychological growth. The first involves the types of relationships that we are able to have with people, and the second is the value of our work to the people around us. The two depend upon each other. For our work to be able to meet the true needs of people, we must be in a close enough relationship with those people to know what their needs are.

BIBLICAL BASE

For the Christian, the issue of fruit is one that goes beyond this life. The Bible suggests that the treasures we store up in heaven are more important than the ones we store up on earth (Matthew 6:19,20). True significance as to the value of one's life can only be determined by God the Father who will be the one to ultimately judge our life's efforts. The non-Christian must accept the reality that human works without faith in God will not lead to salvation. Galatians 2:16 tells us, "Knowing that a man is not justified by the works of the law, but by the faith of Jesus Christ." This suggests that psychologically a person will never experience complete fulfillment in relation to the works that he or she does if those works are separated from a faith in God. True value in our lives only comes as we obtain the eternal life that God the Father gives us when we believe in Jesus Christ as our Lord and Savior. Now that the importance of our faith in God has been established, we must recognize that a true growing faith is one that leads to actions. James 2:17,18 expresses it this way: "Even so faith if it has not works is dead, being by itself. A man may say, you have faith and I have works: show me your faith without your works, and I will show you my faith by my works."

The goal of the Christian, then, is not just to have faith, but to bear spiritual fruit. Christ tells us in John 4:35,36 that we should "Behold, lift up your eyes and look on the fields; for they are white already to harvest. And he that reapeth receives wages and gathers fruit unto eternal life." Also, we are told by Christ in Matthew 7:18–21 that:

> . . . A good tree cannot bring forth evil fruit, nor a corrupt tree good fruit. Every tree that brings not forth good fruit is hewn down and cast into the fire. Wherefore by their fruits you shall know them. Not everyone that says unto me, Lord, Lord, shall enter into the kingdom of heaven; but he that does the will of my Father which is in heaven.

Here we find that we do not produce true fruit leading to eternal life either just by doing human works or by having faith, but by doing the will of God the Father. The will of God the Father, as given to us in the great commandment, is that we love Him with our whole personality and that we love our neighbor as we love ourselves. Through this love and intimacy that we develop in our relationships with God and with people, we will begin to bear fruit. As we allow the love of God to flow through us, other people will be able to experience it too, and they will also begin to love. The message that we carry to the world as Christians is one of God's love for mankind. As we share the love that we have found with people, we will begin to bear the spiritual fruit of that love. As we bear fruit, we are assured of generativity into eternal life through the storing up of treasures in heaven.

Today, many people question God and His Word and refuse to believe in Jesus Christ. They say they do not believe in God and that they can live their lives without Him. Now this is true; it is possible to live one's life while rejecting God and and His commandments. However, it is not possible to escape His judgment. Matthew 12:33 tells us, "For the tree is known by his fruit." Also in Luke 3:9 it states that, "Every tree which bringeth not forth good fruit is hewn down and cast into the fire." That fruit is unrelated to our possessions is confirmed in

I Timothy 6:7 as it informs us, "For we brought nothing into this world and it is certain that we can carry nothing out." That each person will have to stand alone before God and give an accounting is established in I Corinthians 3:8, where it says, "Every man shall receive his own reward according to his own labor." This idea is continued in I Corinthians 3:13–15, as it teaches,

> Every man's work shall be made manifest. For the day shall declare it, because it shall be revealed by fire; and the fire will try every man's work of what sort it is. If a man's work abide which he hath built upon he shall receive a reward. If any man's work shall be burned he shall suffer loss.

Luke 6:43–45 teaches us that the fruit which we produce comes from our heart.

> For a good tree bringeth not forth corrupt fruit; neither doth a corrupt tree bring forth good fruit. For every tree is known by his own fruit. For of thorns men do not gather figs, nor of a bramble bush gather they grapes. A good man out of the good treasure of his heart bringeth forth that which is good; and an evil man out of the evil treasure of his heart bringeth forth that which is evil.

Jesus also tells us that we cannot produce fruit in and of ourselves, but only as we graft ourselves onto the vine—the vine being Jesus Christ. This means that it is impossible for a person who does not have Jesus as their Lord and Savior to produce good fruit as evaluated by God, no matter how many good works he does. This is found in John 15:1–6, where Jesus says:

> I am the true vine and my Father is the husbandman. Every branch in me that beareth not fruit, he taketh away: and every branch that beareth fruit, he purgeth it so that it may bring forth more fruit. . . . Abide in me and I in you. As the branch cannot bear fruit of itself, except it abide in the vine; no more can ye, except ye abide in me. I am the vine and ye are the branches: He that abideth in me, and I in him, the same

bringeth forth much fruit: for without me ye can do nothing. If a man abide not in me he is cast forth as a branch and is withered; and men gather them and cast them into the fire and they are burned.

The conclusion that can be drawn from these Scriptures is that unless our lives produce good fruit we *will not have* eternal life. We also can see that unless Christ is our Lord as well as our Savior we will not be able to produce good fruit. This means that the Lordship of Christ is a necessary part of the salvation process that must be completed by all adults who call themselves Christians or they will not bear good fruit and as a result be cast into the fire and burned. This is confirmed in Matthew 13:37–43, where it says:

> He that soweth the good seed is the Son of man. The field is the world; the good seed are the children of the kingdom; but the tares are the children of the wicked one; the enemy that sowed them is the devil; the harvest is the end of the world; and the reapers are the angels. As therefore the tares are gathered and burned in the fire, so shall it be in the end of this world. The Son of man shall send forth His angels and they shall gather out of his kingdom all things that offend and them which do iniquity; and shall cast them into a furnace of fire: there shall be wailing and gnashing of teeth. Then shall the righteous shine forth as the sun in the kingdom of their Father.

Christianity is neither a game nor a religion. Christianity is a lifetime commitment to the Lordship of Christ and doing the will of God. To the extent that we do this, we will produce good fruit and, thereby, receive eternal life. To the extent that we waver in our faith or become lukewarm in our commitment, our life will produce evil fruit and we will be rejected by God. God will not allow us to live our whole lives choosing the treasures of the world and then receive the treasures of heaven without some sort of repentance. Today many people who call themselves Christians are not truly committed to the cause of Christ, whose lives are not bearing good fruit, and who will not inherit the kingdom of God. "Who hath ears to hear, let him hear" (Matthew 13:43).

HUMAN RESPONSIBILITY

Primary Responsibility

As defined spiritually, the primary responsibility for producing good fruit in the lives of people is on Jesus Christ. Jesus Christ does this through the Holy Spirit which He sends us to teach us how to love. The final judgment as to the type of fruit produced by our lives will be done by God the Father. In this way, the Trinity of the Godhead seeks to work in our lives as adults to conform us to the image of God in which we were created. As we fulfill our potential as created by God through the leading of the Holy Spirit in our lives, our lives develop more than just a human meaning; they also develop an eternal value. This eternal value that our lives take on allows our lives to transcend this physical world and our temporal existence through the granting by God to us of eternal life. The final responsibility for determining the value of our lives will be in the hands of God and not the hands of men. This means that what is written about us in the Book of Life will be more important than what is written about us in the history books of the world.

Although the final judgment of our lives will be made by God, the basis for that judgment will be determined by us. As discussed in earlier chapters, free will means responsibility and free will means accountability. All adults have a free will for which God will hold them accountable whether or not they desire it. Although people may convince the society courts of justice that they were not accountable for their sin, they will not convince God. This means that the secondary responsibility for fruit is in the hands of each individual. Through Jesus Christ and the Holy Spirit, God the Father makes available to every person the potential for bearing good fruit. The responsibility for our failure to do so, however, rests on our shoulders, not God's. The power that we are to use in order to bear good fruit is the power of God's agape love, and this love can only be obtained from God's Holy Spirit. Without agape love, it is impossible to bear fruit. As a result, bearing fruit is not a work of man, whether Christian or non-Christian, but a work of God through man. This is what Jesus meant when He said that He was the vine and we are the branches. Only through Him can we bear good fruit and receive eternal life.

Major Task

The major task during the Fruit Stage is that the older generation of adults *transmit lasting values to the next generation*. Without this transmission of values, society eventually will revert back to the most primitive stage of development—human egocentrism. To the extent that the older adult has completed the steps in the hierarchy of basic human needs, he or she will begin to teach the following generation the way to go. These steps to maturity can be thought of as a roadmap to life. Since the older adult has come to the last stop in the psychospiritual steps of life's growth process, he or she ought to have some insight as to how to get there. The task, then, centers around trying to help succeeding generations to get to the end of the road while making fewer mistakes along the way.

The process assumes that the older adult has completed the hierarchy of basic needs successfully and understands the process enough to teach it to others. In reality, just being older does not necessarily make one wiser. Because of the possibilities of fixation and regression, there are millions of older adults who have not yet successfully found their way to the top of the hierarchy. Needless to say, the older generation cannot teach values that it has not yet experienced or learned. Our conclusion, then, must be that the fewer adults who successfully reach the top of the hierarchy of basic needs, the fewer who will be able to show younger generations the way successfully. From a psychological perspective, the psychospiritual health of any society will be determined by how high on the hierarchy of basic human needs the majority of adults will have reached. Today, an evaluation of our society would lead to the conclusion that over the last forty years our country has been regressing in terms of its overall psychospiritual development. This has led to an increase in individual psychological sickness and the beginning onset of social chaos.

Technique

If, as we have established, the major task during the Fruit Stage is the transmission from one generation to the next of substantive, lasting values, the older generation is required to have learned what these true values are. The process whereby one discovers true values is through a true understanding of life and the developmental steps of life. The technique used is one of *developing wisdom*. Many people, young and old, have knowledge. However, knowledge alone cannot save us or the society within which we live. As a philosophy, secular humanism builds itself on rational thinking and human reasoning. The leaders of this movement are scholars in that they have vast stores of knowledge in their minds. But can we get wisdom merely by having knowledge? In psychology, the assumption is that truth can be and will be discovered about man strictly through empirical methods of gathering data. In this way, the whole merely becomes the sum of its parts.

However, the Bible teaches that man through rational thinking and the gathering of data will never be able to comprehend fully the wonders of the universe and the wonders of man. It says that those who seek their final truth through knowledge do not become wise, but are merely fools. They deny the existence of God and the wonder of His creation and, as a result, merely teach the thoughts of man. On the other hand, true wisdom must come from God through a belief in God. Since God created the universe and man, He is to be the source of its secrets revealed. In other words, for the older generation to transmit lasting values to the next generation, they must have wisdom. While knowledge comes from the books of men and only a small percentage can be scholars, wisdom comes from the Word of God and every one is capable of becoming wise. To be wise is to know the truth and the truth is to be found in the Bible.

Focal Point

Once a person has discovered the truth and developed wisdom, he has a responsibility to *pass it on*. One of the problems in our churches today is that we are placing too much of the responsibility for passing on the truth upon the pastor and young adults. The problem here is that, although the young adult may intellectually know the truth of God's Word, he or she does not yet really know it experientially. Christianity needs more older adults who are willing to share from their life experiences the reality of God's blessings and importance of human faith. It is not the young adult who has been given the primary responsibility for the transmission of wisdom to the next generation, but the older adult. When young adults are put in charge, they focus too much on knowledge because, for lack of experience, they have too little wisdom. What is needed is an army of older Christians who will rise up and begin to share from their hearts what God has meant to their lives. The group that would probably be helped most by this would be our confused, searching teenagers. If Christ has meant something to the older adult, then, they need to tell people about it and pass it on.

Goal of Stage

The end product of this life-long quest for wisdom that can then be passed on to following generations is a better world in which we can live. In saying this, we are assuming that a life lived by the truth is more fulfilling and brings more happiness than one based on lies. In terms of love, our conclusion is that God's agape love in one's life will be better than cheap substitutes such as sex or romance. In terms of psychological health, we can say that we will have less conflict in our lives if we learn to face and cope with reality than if we try to deny it or run from it. The wise person, then, is an older adult who has come to be known as *one who sought and found the truth about life*. The wise person does not just tell people the truth, he or she lives it. If our Christian walk with God is supposed to bring a deeper happiness to our lives, then our life ought to reflect that happiness. Young people do not consider those who say one thing and live something else as wise, but hypocrites. What is needed today from the generation of older Christians is more wisdom and less hypocrisy. This can only be accomplished through a real relationship with God and a faith that is planted on the firm foundation of Jesus Christ and God's Word.

PSYCHOLOGICAL NEED

Basic Need

The basic human need from our hierarchy during the Fruit Stage is for *value*. We all want to be able to look back on our lives and feel like there was some meaning to our existence. No one wants to believe that the effort one put into struggling through all of the conflicts and stresses of life was futile. Meaning, then, reasserts itself in a new way during the Fruit Stage. The crisis of meaning associated with the Meaning Stage was based on idealism and what one hoped to be and do. Meaning, as value during the Fruit Stage, is based on realism and a reflection of what one has done. By the time a person reaches the Fruit Stage, he or she must eventually face and come to grips with the third crisis of adult life, which is the *crisis of death*. The crisis of death centers around the fear older adults have that they will die before they do something truly meaningful with their lives and as a result their lives will have no value.

There are four primary areas in which people attempt to find and establish value in their lives. The first of these is in the area of *work*. Some people attempt to meet their need for value through their job or work role. If they feel like their job has human and social value, they will feel satisfied with the sacrifices and stresses they must bear in relation to their work. If people do not feel like the formal work they are doing has value, they will become unhappy and dissatisfied with their jobs. One way of measuring work satisfaction is in terms of how much the worker focuses on money. The more value a person experiences in relation to his or her vocation, the less that money will be an important variable. The less value a person perceives in relation to the value of his or her work, the more that he will focus on money. In this way, a materialistic society is built out of that society's inability to create meaningful work experiences for its people. One of the virtues of Christianity is that commitment to the cause of Christ makes all work more meaningful since it gives it greater value.

The second area in which people seek to create value in their life is in their *family*. Some people who do not feel that their work itself has value create value out of it as it becomes the means by which they provide for the needs of their family. It is this sense of duty to one's family that creates the incentive to continue at a job that is considered hard or unrewarding. Fulfillment for these people does not come at work, then, but at home. As a result, when work is over these people seek to escape it as quickly as possible and return to the family. These people feel most fulfilled as they give things to or do things with family members. Conflict arises when family members do not seem to show appreciation for the sacrifices that were made. When this happens, the person who tries to find value through his family will begin to experience frustration and may become angry or depressed. The problem is that this person tried to obtain value by living through family members. Christianity creates value in our families, not as we need each other, but as we love each other.

The third area in which some people attempt to establish value for their lives is in *social involvement*. Social involvement includes those activities that people do for which they do not get paid but which they feel will lead to the betterment of their community, their country, or their world. Social involvement arises out of a sense of social responsibility. The goal is to make the world a better place in which to live and the hope is that it will give one's life value. Hours of time are spent by people raising money for charity, being involved in service projects in a community, serving on boards of organizations, and supervising young people in their skill development. Since there is no salary for most of these people, it is something other than money that causes them to give of their time in this way. Again, it is the hope that such activity will give one's life added meaning and value which creates the incentive for this activity. As Christians, part of our commitment to the cause of Christ must include the social needs of those around us. Christians should try to reflect God's love in their community by being socially involved.

A fourth area in which many people invest a significant amount of time, energy, and money is in their *religious involvement*. In the same way that some people attempt to create value in their life through involvement in their community, others try to find value through their involvement in their religious organization or church. In this case, value is determined by how well one follows the traditions of that religious organization based upon that organization's concept of God. Value comes as one's life and lifestyle are brought into conformity with the stated religious goals and teachings. To the extent that individuals are not able to live up to their stated religious strivings, they will feel like their lives have not had value, since they have failed to live up to the religious standards expected of them. Although Christians are religious, Christianity is to be more than a religion. Religion is a system of works used to earn value. Christianity is a system of love used to reflect value.

As Christians, we should not seek to escape our responsibilities in these four areas of our lives—work, family, social involvement, and church involvement. However, we need to understand that by themselves none of these things can give value to our lives. Value does not come to our lives through our works, but through our fruit. *Works* can be defined as *the right behavior which we perform or do in order to earn the love of men and of God.* Through works, we attempt to measure the value of our lives through the materialistic possessions that we have obtained, the accomplishments we have completed, and the awards or status we have been given. The problem is that none of these can give lasting value to our life. *Fruit,* on the other hand, is defined as the *righteous living which we reflect because of the power of God's love operating through us.* Fruit is determined strictly on the basis of the lives that we have touched. If our lives have touched the lives of others, whether it be at work, at home, in our community, or through our church, in such a way that God's love has been able to change them, we will have produced good fruit. If, on the other hand, through our lives people have been led away from God's love or been caused to reject God's love, our life will have produced evil fruit.

The positive emotion that results in our life as we are able to bear good fruit through the sharing of God's love is *unity.* Unity in a marriage is referred to in the Bible as "one flesh" and comes as the two people are able to share God's love together. Unity in the church is referred to as fellowship. This results when a specific group of Christians are able to put their primary focus on their common bond in Christ. As we find true value in our lives, then, we will be able to experience the positive emotional state of unity or oneness with our fellowman in all four areas of our lives. To the extent that we neglect any one of the four areas associated with value, our lives become out of balance and our sense of unity is destroyed.

Psychological State

The psychological state that results when we are able to bear good fruit and meet our human need for value is one of *transcendence*. As we share God's love with people in all the areas of our lives, His love is able to reproduce itself into the lives of others. In this way, our lives transcend themselves by multiplying themselves in future generations. True transcendence, then, does not come on the physical plane through human procreation, but on the spiritual plane through spiritual reproduction. More important than having a child is the raising of that child, and more important than the child's physical needs are his or her psychospiritual needs. As we read the Bible, we see that all of the people of the world are God's children and every adult is capable of spiritual reproduction. It is only through spiritual reproduction that our lives are able to gain true transcendence as we store up fruit for eternal life.

Self-Esteem

True self-esteem, then, during the Fruit Stage stems from the impact that our lives have had on the lives of others. This is contrary to what most young adults believe, which is that self-esteem in old age will be determined by what one has accomplished. Individuals reach the Fruit Stage when they begin to see the emptiness of their accomplishments. The problem with accomplishments is that they focus on self and what one is doing for self. The desire is that people will look at us and what we have accomplished and be impressed. To try to obtain self-esteem through our personal accomplishments is not a step forward in the developmental process but a step backwards to the Behavior Stage. It was in the Behavior Stage that people had a need for competency. The Christian solution to this problem of self-esteem tied to performance was to discover that God is not interested in our being the best, but only in our doing our best. As adults, doing our best should no longer be an area in which we feel a need for attention and recognition. Instead, by the time we reach middle adulthood the focus should be on meeting the basic needs of others. In doing this, we will bear fruit and our lives will have value. Self-esteem in the Fruit Stage, then, is related to *being remembered for what we are doing or have done for others* and not to what we have accomplished for self.

HUMAN FALL

As in all of the previous stages, every person will at some point experience a marring in his or her development in terms of the Fruit Stage. Until we learn to understand it and deal with it through the power of God, sin continues to be a force in our lives that reasserts itself whenever we are faced with a new developmental task. The primary problem that everyone must face, including Christian adults as well as non-Christian adults, is the crisis of death. The crisis of death comes when we begin to sense our mortality and the short nature of our physical existence. In the crisis of death, people begin to feel that life is passing them by, that because of age and the aging process they are being left behind. The crisis of death begins to affect people when their past looks better than their future, when life's best experiences have already been experienced and the future seems to offer only frustration and pain. It comes to a person when the direction of his or her career seems to be only a downward one. It comes to people when parenting seems to be over and the children are grown. The crisis of death, then, is associated with the idea that it is just about all over and that there is not much significant left to do. The focal point of this psychospiritual concern is the very fact of physical death itself, which is made worse by friends and loved ones who are actually dying.

In reality, physical life is relatively short when measured by eternity, and most people as they approach the end do not want to leave or let go. Most middle-aged adults do not like the idea of growing old. Aging, therefore, becomes an enemy to be conquered or a reality to be denied. The truth, however, is that no one will beat death on the physical plane. We can fight it or we can deny it, but we cannot stop it. If people in middle age do not accept the process of aging and the reality of physical death, they will begin to experience psychological stress and conflict in their lives. There are various techniques that are used to resist the reality of the crisis of death, but in the end none of them work. Examples might include a middle-aged woman getting a face lift or coloring her hair blond in order to look younger, or a middle-aged man discarding his wife and replacing her with a twenty-year-old substitute to prove he's still "got it." What both of these people still have that can never be escaped is the fact that they are middle-aged. As Christians we may, in the process of growth, struggle with the reality of death, but we do not have to be afraid of it. Through Christ, we are able to have victory over death and life beyond the grave, and this should be cause for rejoicing.

Negative Cognitive State

The negative cognitive state that arises when we produce evil fruit rather than good fruit is *isolation*. By middle adulthood, if we were a stumbling block to those people to which we were the closest, they will begin to move away from us. Children as children must put up with the selfishness, emotional pathology, and abuse of parents because without some outside intervention it is very difficult to escape their control. However, there comes a point when the child grows up and is able to leave. If a parent had an evil effect on the child's life, the child will not return. Eventually the person finds him- or herself alone and isolated—all those who were considered loved ones are gone and those who were rejected now reject in return. This means that the failure to give love in our thirties and forties leads to a failure to be loved in our fifties and sixties.

The resultant negative emotion that eventually arises out of this state of isolation is *futility*. Like the author of the book of Eccelesiastes in the Bible, a person comes to say "vanity of vanity; all is vanity (Ecclesiates 1:2)." Futility leads to the questions of what was it all for and what did it all mean. For the person who only lived for self and refused to love and care about people, life is senseless and has no meaning. Not only will this person experience the state of isolation and the emotion of futility now on a temporal basis, they will also experience it later, after God's judgment, as they spend an eternity in hell. Futility as an emotion is not primarily associated with being a failure in life, but comes instead through being a success. Futility comes when we reach our goals and still feel empty and unfulfilled. What we find is that the things of the world—possessions, status, and awards—that we try so hard to obtain never really give the full satisfaction that we expected after we get them.

Primary Fear

The primary fear associated with the Fruit Stage and the crisis of death is the fear that life is about over and *I missed my chance*. The reason many people try so hard to hold onto life is because they are dissatisfied with what they did with it. Most people look back on their lives and see a battleground. The highest virtue of it is that they survived, but even in this area the victory was only temporary. Life ought to be something more than survival. God meant that we should live life and enjoy life, not just endure it. The fear that we missed our chance carries with it the harsh reality that the dreams and hopes of youth were never realized or fulfilled and probably never will be. For most people, then, living as a whole becomes a depressing experience where what you get never quite comes up to the expectations of what you wanted. The first few times we feel this way as adults, we just try harder to find the happiness we seek through the things of the world. Eventually, though, a person comes to feel it's over; it's too late to attain that happiness; I had my chance and I blew it.

Existential Sin

Whenever people feel that there is no longer any reason to struggle, to try, or to change, they commit the final sin in the developmental sequence—they *harden their heart to God.* God is capable of teaching us and changing us up to the very second that we physically die. Salvation is available and possible until this physical body takes its last breath. No one is so lost that he or she cannot be found by God. No one is so evil that Christ's blood cannot atone for him or her. All that is needed is for the person to yield and repent. Once a person dies, however, the chances are over. Far too many people who have many years of usefulness left in their lives have given up too soon. As these people give up through an acceptance of their state of isolation and sense of futility, they harden their hearts toward God's Holy Spirit. When this happens, God's love can no longer break through. In this way, people first reject the love of others and then eventually reject the love of God. To reject God's love and the symbol of it—His Son Jesus Christ—is to commit the unpardonable sin. It is impossible for people to dwell eternally in the presence of God's love when they have rejected it their whole lives. In other words, to reject God's love is to reject God; to reject God's love is to produce evil fruit; and to reject God's love is to bring God's judgment upon us.

The neurotic fantasy that accompanies hardening our heart toward God is the boastful claim that *I did it my way and I have no regrets.* Sadly, this person, after he or she is in hell, will have plenty of regrets. The only problem is that then it will be too late. Many who while physically alive live lives of pleasure and immorality. They do what they please, they use people, they take the name of God in vain, and they brag about it. They defy God and challenge God and think that because God does not immediately punish them that they have beaten God. No one beats God; not even Satan. Everyone will stand before God and His judgment. There will be no exceptions. These boasters will not be bragging then, but crying out in fear. Their cries, however, will not be heard; it will be too late. For those who feel they have missed their chance, do not harden your heart to God. It is not too late. God loves you and is willing to give you eternal life; all you must do is ask and believe.

FRUIT STAGE

Human Responsibility

Primary Responsibility	**God**
Major Task	To transmit lasting values to the next generation.
Technique	**Develop wisdom**
Focal Point	**Pass it on**
Goal	To be known as one who sought and found the truth about life.

Psychological Need

Basic Need	**Value**
Resultant Positive Emotion	**Unity**
Psychological State	**Transcendence**
Self-Esteem	I am **remembered** for what I have contributed to society.

Human Fall

Negative Cognitive State	**Isolation**
Resultant Negative Emotion	**Futility**
Primary Fear	**I missed my chance.**
Existential Sin	**Hardened heart**
Neurotic Fantasy	I did it my way and I have no regrets.

12
Finding the Will of God

It is a very common occurrence to find young adults who are having struggles and conflicts as Christians in terms of what God would have them do with their lives. Many of these young adults feel that their inability to establish a clearly defined path for their lives is somehow a reflection of a lack of spirituality on their part or a lack of concern on God's part. The expectation seems to be that the normal procedure is for God to give young adults a well-defined audible call by the time they are twenty that tells them what job He wants them to take or which career to pursue. If a person has reached twenty-five without receiving such a direct calling, there must be something wrong with that person's spiritual condition.

In Christian circles, then, there are two groups of young people which we will label the "haves" and the "have-nots." The former are those who say that they have received some kind of special revelation of God directing them in their major life decisions, while the latter are those young adults who feel confused because they have not received any clear direction from God and they are wondering why. The problem comes when Christian preachers and teachers seem to value a clear call by age twenty more highly than an ongoing search, and present this as the norm. In reality, most young adult Christians do not have any clear sense of what God wants them to do with their lives, and those who claim a mystical revelation of God's will are a very small minority. Even many of those who at twenty felt that their lives were totally set and planned find that by thirty many changes had to be made along the way.

Today it is very unusual to find someone at fifty in the same job that they started at twenty-five. And the prediction is that this generation of young adults will be making more changes in their career development than their parents' generation, not less. The question with which we are faced, then, concerns how we are to go about helping Christian young people understand God's will in terms of life choices in this fast-changing world. The two most important choices that need to be dealt with are those of vocation and marriage. The problem comes as the young adult's satisfaction with the choices is not measuring up to their expectations in both marriage and work. By allowing God's stamp of approval to be put prematurely on choices that are really made by self, we run the risk of having the blame projected onto God when these choices do not work out the way we expected.

This chapter begins with the premise, therefore, that we have presented to our young people the idea of seeking God's will in a very superficial way. Actually, the discovering of God's will for one's life must be viewed as a life-long process. This process will have different areas of focus, depending upon which developmental stage we are in at the time. No one at twenty can anticipate all of the factors that will affect his or her life and the choices that will be made. The first step, then, in finding the will of God is to accept the fact that we cannot find the will of God on a long-term basis except as it is revealed in His Word. In other words, the Christian walk is a walk of faith where each day we learn to seek His leading and guidance. It is the fallen nature, the flesh within us, that wants to have our whole life planned ahead of time and insecurity of choice eliminated. To succumb to this fleshly desire to plan our whole lives is a sin and our walk is no longer one of faith. Faith means that we must trust God for the tomorrows that we cannot see rather than being anxious because we do not know what lies ahead.

USING THE WORD OF GOD

To find the will of God, the first thing the young adult must do is learn the Word of God. Since there are many other books that deal extensively with how to use God's Word to understand and cope with daily living, we only will discuss it briefly here. Many Christians still seek supernatural revelations of God's will in relation to a particular decision or problem that is already covered in His Word. God expects us to know what His Word says and to live our lives accordingly. One question, for example, that sometimes arises in counseling concerns whether or not God wants a person to get a divorce. In this case, prayer will not lead to the answer because the question is already answered in God's Word at Mark 10:9, where it says, "What, therefore, God hath joined together let not man put asunder." This means that, although God accepts the reality of divorce, it is never His will that two people make this choice, but theirs.

Another good example of using God's Word to find God's will is found in I Thessalonians 5:16–18, where we are told to "Rejoice evermore, pray without ceasing, in everything give thanks: for this is the will of God in Christ Jesus concerning you." This particular passage instructs us that rejoicing, praying, and thanking God are all to be parts of our daily walk with God. Too many Christians fail to fulfill these commands and then wonder why God seems so far away. When life does not go the way we want and we become angry or frustrated, it is not God who moves away from us, but we who move away from God. As we can thank God in everything and rejoice in the face of our problems, Satan loses his ability to control our attitude as we remain in fellowship with God. In conclusion, it is important as Christians that we learn to follow and live by what we know God wants us to do because it is recorded in His Word before we begin to seek some special solution to our problems and choices. The answers to most of the questions we have and problems we face can be found recorded in His Word. What we must do is discover what His Word says and then be willing to obey and follow it.

BECOMING A MAN OF GOD

The second general issue that we must deal with in finding God's will for our life concerns where God places the focus of attention. In Christian discussions we often focus merely on the works component as the primary determinant of fulfilling God's will. In this situation the attention is placed on what we are doing for God, and our spiritual maturity is evaluated by our behavior. The Bible clearly teaches, as we have already discussed in this book, that our fruit is more important to God than our works and that people are more important than possessions. It is the natural response of man to evaluate and judge himself and his peers on the basis of the external elements of our human experience—namely, our actions or behaviors. In this framework, young people seeking God's will continue to ask the question as to *What does God want me to do?*

In reality, God's first concern is not in our doing, in terms of our works, but in our becoming, in terms of our growth. The real question we need to be asking God is *What does He want me to be?* The young adult wants to have the job and responsibilities of a mature adult without going through the process of growth. Whenever we try to do for God before we become a man or woman of God, what we do always ends up being for self. This means that in the first half of our adult life God is more concerned about our psychospiritual growth than He is about our worldly success. The problem for us as humans is that we want success to be easy and we do not want to experience psychological conflict or be asked to make psychospiritual changes in order to obtain it. In the end, we will not be able to find God's will for our lives without being willing to make psychospiritual changes in ourselves, and these changes need to take place before we achieve success. Any success we obtain before we make these changes will end up being for self and not for God.

Second, God is more concerned about what we are like on the inside than what we are like on the outside. The Bible indicates that it is man who judges on the basis of what he sees in terms of human behavior, but God judges us by what is in our hearts (I Samuel 16:7). To find the will of God for our lives, we need to see that God wants us to get a right heart before we concern ourselves with right behavior. This does not mean that God is not concerned about right behavior. It merely means that, for God, right behavior is not enough. Christianity does not begin as a behavior or action that we do or perform but as a commitment of the heart that we make. This principle is true throughout our whole lives. God is always more concerned about a right heart than He is about right behavior. As we have a right heart the right behavior will come, but it will be because of love and not because of guilt.

UNDERSTANDING THE CALL OF GOD

The biggest problem that we have had in trying to seek or define the call of God for any given Christian is a lack of understanding of the developmental stages. In the past, we have viewed adulthood as one big stage. Today, we are discovering more and more that adulthood, like childhood, must be broken down into stages, or steps, each with its own development task and crisis. The implication for our discussion here is that we need to see the call of God in its developmental context. In the past, Christians have taken the view that the call of God only comes once, usually early in adult life, and we must spend the rest of our lives fulfilling this early call. In this section we will present a new conceptualization, which is that the call of God comes to us in a progressive sequence that has three distinct components or steps. We will refer to these steps in the process as the General Call, the Role Call, and the Special Call.

The General Call of God is found in Matthew 28:19,20, when it commands Christians to,

> Go ye therefore and teach (make disciples of) all nations, baptizing them in the name of the Father, and of the Son, and of the Holy Spirit: teaching them to observe all things whatsoever I have commanded you: and lo I am with you always even unto the end of the world.

This passage is commonly referred to as the Great Commission. In the developmental process this Great Commission comes when we leave the wilderness or Unstage of life. We do this by making Christ Lord of our life, taking self off the throne of our heart and putting Christ on it. This leads us to the Meaning Stage, where we find true meaning in life by making a total commitment to the cause of Christ. As we make Christ Lord of our life, we become responsible to Christ for utilizing our abilities and talents to fulfill Christ's Great Commission to spread the Gospel to the whole world. For any person who is attempting to call themselves a Christian and seek God's will who has not made Christ Lord of his life, God will be silent. God will not give direction to any person's life until that person first makes a total commitment to God through the Lordship of Christ. Discovering the call of God, then, begins with a commitment to the cause of Christ.

This General Call in the form of the Great Comission comes at the end of the Unstage, which we confront somewhere between the ages of fifteen and twenty-five. A common problem in Christian circles, however, is that we commonly misinterpret the General Call that is experienced by our Christian young people during this time. We have equated our responsibility to fulfill the Great Commission with an additional vocational commitment to be in full-time Christian service. In reality, the General Call to fulfill the Great Commission is for all Christian young people under the Lordship of Christ. The command to take the Gospel of Christ to the world is not optional for the committed Christian, but a requirement. The Bible clearly tells us that this command or call to the Great Commission is universal to all Christians.

This means that at this point in the developmental process every Christian is called to full-time Christian service. It also means that every Christian young adult at twenty is called to preach, called to be a minister, and called to be a missionary. There are no exceptions. At the same time, it also means that the call to preach at the end of the Unstage is not a unique call, reserved only for a few special Christians, and has nothing to do with a young person's vocation. The General Call, therefore, is a universal call to all Christian young adults to take the Gospel message of Christ to the world. Regardless of the vocation or role that young adults choose to fill in society, they are all in full-time Christian service. For committed Christian young adults, there is no such thing as a secular vocation.

A second aspect of the General Call is that it is to be based on a concept of spiritual equality. It is neither our talents and abilities nor our human efforts at serving God that save us. God does not want our works; He wants us so that He can work through us. Although salvation requires that we have faith, it is still a work of God's grace through the blood of Jesus Christ. We come to God, therefore, with nothing at the end of the Unstage. In this way, we all start spiritually equal. As Christians, we are not to think of competing with our fellow Christians for the attention and favor of God. Neither are we to think of ourselves as more important to God than some other Christian because we have talents that they do not have. We do not please God by making ourselves more successful in the ministry than someone else. God will not judge us on the basis of how we did in relation to others, but on the basis of how we did in relation to our potential. The competition, then, for the Christian is only with self and not with others. Problems arise only when we begin to think that it is *our abilities* that God needs to spread the Gospel when it is really *our availability*.

The final aspect of the General Call concerns the burden that we obtain along with it for people and the world. To be independent is to be responsible and to be responsible is to be willing to shoulder part of the burden for the needs of others. As we attempt to do our part to fulfill the Great Commission, we must begin to look beyond ourselves and see a world of people who are suffering physically, psychologically, and spiritually. Through the General Call, we begin to have a vision of reaching out to a lost world and begin to experience a burden for helping to fulfill Christ's command. Again our tendency is to overinterpret what this burden means. We tend to assume that to have a burden for the world is the same thing as having love for people. The problem is that for the young adult this burden for the world is abstract. We must be willing to let God redefine the burden in a concrete way, through the developmental process. In reality, the young adult needs to discover that the true measure of his or her ability to love the whole world is his or her ability to love one person who seems unlovable. God wants us to see that it is empty words to claim that we love people who we do not know when we cannot love people who we do know. Our conclusion, then, must be that having a burden and loving people are two different things. In the developmental process, the young adult who experiences the General Call of God to full-time Christian service receives a burden for the world but will need to learn how to love people before that burden can be channeled into a form that is useable by God.

The Role Call

In the last section, it was suggested that the General Call of God comes at the end of the Unstage as we make Christ Lord of our life. This leads the young adult into the Meaning Stage, where he or she seeks to find meaning and purpose for life. In the chapter on Meaning it was suggested that, initially, the primary way that all people seek to establish meaning is through the roles that are taken on in society. It was suggested that eventually each person must learn that it is not the role that gives life meaning, but what you do with it. For young adults who have not yet fully discovered the meaning and power of God's love, all they can do is choose to fill a role. This means that during their twenties Christian young adults are doing nothing more than choosing and learning to play a role. Even within the playing of social roles we are to seek to do the will of God, which means that during this time God seeks to call us to roles and to learn to operate within their boundaries.

Problems arise, however, due to the idealism of youth. Young adults want to do more than play a role; they want to change the world and reach their goals now. Patience is not one of the primary virtues of young adults in their twenties. Conflicts arise when the idealism of a burden or vision for God confronts the reality of people's unwillingness to change or respond. An even greater problem for young adults is that they are still viewed many times as children whose ideas just will not work. It is within the roles that we choose during this time of life that idealism challenges reality and more often than not loses. This is within God's plan. God wants our initial vision as a young adult to be destroyed because it is through our disillusionment upon the destruction of our dreams for our life that God can build His. God's will is that our love for the world become concrete, not abstract. God's will is that we follow His plan for our lives and not our own.

As a result, God's will for our Role Call only comes through objective, rational evaluation of what we would like to do and what we are capable of doing. God will not call someone to fill the role of a doctor who does not have the intellectual abilities to pass the entrance examination. God will not call someone to fill the role of being someone's wife who does not choose to ask her out for a date. God will not call someone to be a professional athlete who cannot make the team. In terms of our Role Call then, God will not call us to do something that we cannot do or do not desire to do. God wants us to search for our role within the boundaries of our abilities and interests. However, too many young adults seek God's Role Call as a mystical or supernatural revelation. They want and expect God to reveal to them in some magical way who to marry, what college to attend, what major to take, and/or what job to seek. God will not do any of these things on a regular basis in such a way that it would cut short the process of growth. Too often we seek supernatural revelations as acts of faith, which only reflects to God a lack of faith on our part in His ability to direct our lives.

The focus, then, during the Meaning Stage, as we seek God's Role Call, should be on making *good choices, not perfect ones.* As stated before, young adults are impatient. They want to fill the shoes of an older adult and receive the recognition without going through the pain involved in the growth process. We call this understanding of the true reality of life's struggles wisdom and find that true wisdom only comes through experience. While young people today may have more knowledge than their elders, they usually have less wisdom. The first bit of wisdom that all young adults need to learn and accept is that you cannot operate in the world as if you are forty-five when you are only twenty-five. The desire of the young adult is to make a choice, either in relation to marriage or vocation, that would allow them to skip part of the developmental process. This is not within God's plan. There are no perfect marriages, and there are no perfect jobs. The Christian young adult needs to seek a good spouse or a good job and not a perfect one. Our desire to find perfection is not based upon God's will but upon human neurotic need. The question that we must ask concerns how one is to find perfection in such choices when the person is still imperfect.

There is a danger for Christianity if we encourage our young adults to seek perfect choices; it is the problem of elitism. As we allow some young people to claim that the role that they are choosing to fill is more important to God than some other role, we create within them the potential for false piety. In reality, the role that a person chooses to fill does not make that person more spiritually mature or wise. Maturity and wisdom are associated with spiritual growth, not with the role one plays. In other words, just because a person chooses to fill the role of the pastor of a church, by itself, does not guarantee that that person has the attributes needed to be a spiritually mature pastor. Second, the role that a person chooses does not determine that person's spiritual worth or value to God. As previously stated, our value to God comes as we fulfill our potential and not through the filling of a role. This means that no Role Call during this stage of life is more important than any other.

The goal of this time of life is to learn to fill our role well. There are three main things that young people need to focus on during the first half of their adult life in order to be ready for the third call in the last half of adult life. The first is *credentials*. Christian young adults should shoot for as high as they can go within a realistic assessment of their abilities. Credentials develop from training and education. As Christians, we should attempt to seek the most and best training that we can get. By obtaining good credentials, we will have greater opportunities to serve the Lord. Whatever role we choose to take, we should try to be at least as well qualified for it as those with whom we will be competing in the secular world.

The second area of focus during this time is *competency*. Competency comes after we get a job, not through the training for it. Again, as Christians, we should be known by the world as people who work hard and seek excellency in what we are doing. There is no virtue in being second rate in our roles. In fact, laziness and lack of dedication become factors that block our ability to share our faith. Through competency, we can gain the respect of the world, which eventually makes it possible for us to share the Gospel with it.

The third area that must be dealt with is *credibility*. No one considers young adults to be experts in anything, no matter how much they know. Credibility only comes through experience, and experience only comes through time. Young adults must be patient and wait for the time when they will have the mantle passed to them by the older generation. Too many young adults want the mantle now and try to get it by taking it. This will not work. The mantle of credibility and expertise only comes through our faithfulness to the task and not our desire to be famous.

Special Call

The Special Call of God comes in the Fruit Stage somewhere in middle adulthood. Within the plan of God is a Special Call for every Christian. This Special Call is just as universal as the General Call and goes beyond our ability to envision. It is a special ministry that is *unique* to each individual Christian—meaning that it is something meant by God for only that individual. Several defining characteristics to this Special Call of God are:

1. It cannot be planned or anticipated early in our adult life.
2. It leads us to a higher plane of Christian commitment and service, even for those who already were in "full-time" Christian service.

3. It utilizes all of our potential.
4. It requires us to take a risk or step of faith.
5. It must be unique to the individual in that it would include a special burden, a special group of people, and a special message.

The Special Call is placed in the Fruit Stage because it cannot be received until we first truly learn the meaning of God's love and develop the ability to care about and love people. This means that although God has a Special Call for every Christian, most will not receive one because they have not learned how to love (I Corinthians 13). The only way that we will be able to obtain God's Special Call for our life is through the successful mastery of all of life's developmental stages. By the time we reach the Fruit Stage, God no longer wants to use our role to produce fruit, He wants to use us. In this stage, however, God cannot produce fruit through us unless we have learned to become channels for His love. This means that the first spiritual gift that any Christian can obtain from God is love.

Today, many Christians are seeking to discover the specific spiritual gifts that God promised in the Bible to give us. There is much confusion among young adults as to the nature and process of how to go about figuring the specific spiritual gifts that one has. God will not develop our other spiritual gifts until we first develop our gift of love. The first and most important gift of God is His love and without it everything else is meaningless. In our developmental theory, love was a much later developing concept than we thought in that we placed its origin in the mid-twenties and said that it took several years to learn how to love successfully. If the first spiritual gift that all Christians obtain from God is love, we will not discover our special or unique spiritual gifts until the Fruit Stage. This means that it is ridiculous and misleading to attempt to help young adults to discover their spiritual gifts since they cannot be discovered during young adulthood. Instead, our spiritual gifts are associated with our Special Calling and will not manifest themselves until middle adulthood. The so-called gifts that many Christians claim to have before this time in life are really either talents, which they have always had, or pseudo-gifts given to them by Satan.

GOD'S PLAN FOR GREATNESS

God's Curve Versus Man's Curve

There are two different patterns or curves that can be used as the blueprint for one's life. The first is man's curve, which seeks happiness, success, and psychological health on the basis of immediacy—the sooner I get these things the better. The young adult attempting to go through life using man's curve sees life as an obstacle course that must be overcome and a competition to be won. In other words, the fastest people through the course are the winners and those who go slowly are losers. The second path of life is God's curve. God's curve also focuses on the issues of happiness, success, and psychological health, but speed is not the primary virtue. In this case, life is not a race to be run, but a trip to be enjoyed and appreciated. From this perspective, we can see that those who try to get to the end of the trip too fast miss out on much of the beauty of the journey. What we discover as we examine people's lives is that those who live by man's curve and store up treasures on earth usually reach their peak in middle adulthood and the rest of life is a gradual downhill slide. On the other hand, those who attempt to live by God's curve and store up treasures in heaven may seem to have less in the first half of adulthood, but end up having more in the last half. The following diagrams represent our two curves.

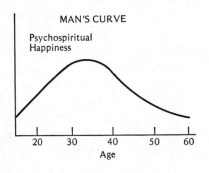

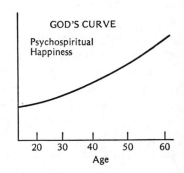

Differences
in the Two Curves

The first difference in the two curves is that man's curve views life as a sprint while God's curve views life as a distance race. Using man's curve, the focus is upon how fast you are running, especially in the early parts of the race. Using God's curve, the focus is upon pacing yourself so that you successfully can run the whole race. The real question concerns where the finish line is located. If life really is a sprint, it is wise to run fast and try to be a success by thirty-five. However, if life is really a distance run, it would be foolish to use up all of your energy in the first ten years and then burn out.

The second difference between the two curves is that man's curve is based upon the idea that goals are more important than people, while God's curve is based upon the idea that people are more important than goals. The secular man views people as hurdles to be overcome or sources of manipulation to be used to reach one's goals. The secular man also uses people as scapegoats to be blamed when goals are not reached and success is not obtained. The man of God views loving people as the number one goal of life and values human relationships more highly than human success or human possessions. In focusing on self the secular man makes people his enemies, while in focusing on others the man of God makes people his friends. Life is more fulfilling in the second half of adult life if we make friends rather than enemies of people in the first half.

The third difference between those who live by man's curve and those who live by God's curve is in family relationships. The person who seeks money, status, and possessions as indications of success in young adulthood usually spends much less time with his or her family. The person's marriage and family are taken for granted and the focus is on giving things to family members. The person who seeks God's will places family as a higher priority than success. Family relationships are cultivated through time spent together. This person is more concerned about giving family members love than in giving them things. The secular man uses his money in an attempt to buy the love of his family, while the Christian man uses his time to share love with his family.

Again, the family relationships of the secular man tend to deteriorate in middle adulthood while those of the person living by God's curve tend to become more fulfilling.

The fourth difference in the two curves is that man's curve seeks to store up treasures on earth while God's curve leads us to store up treasures in heaven. Using man's curve, success is evaluated on the basis of getting the things of the world that are temporal, such as an expensive house, an important job, a high salary, fame, power, and social status. The problem with these things is that just as quickly as we obtain them we can lose them—they are not lasting. On the other hand, using God's curve, success is based on a standard such that all people can obtain it. Success as determined by God is based on the fruits of our life, and fruit represents the people that we have touched with our life. Not everyone can be rich and famous, but everyone can learn to care and share.

The fifth and final difference between the two curves is that man's curve only leads one to be great for self, while God's curve leads us to be great for God. This whole book dealing with God's psychospiritual stages of human development is based on the idea that, since God created us, God's way is the best way. This means that being great for God will in the long run be more fulfilling and bring greater happiness than trying to be great for self.

How to Produce Fruit

If producing good fruit is the ultimate goal of life and the only road to true greatness, we need to concentrate more as we go through life on the type of fruit that we are producing. We will close this chapter with two final concrete suggestions that will help people to live a more fruitful life and in doing that find God's will for their life.

First, we should try at all times to keep our life in balance. Psychological and spiritual problems begin to develop in our lives when we invest too much time and energy in only one part of it. We must have time for self, family, friends, work, and God. Any time we begin to neglect one or more of these areas of our life, our life gets out of balance and we have problems. The psychospiritually healthy adult is one who is able to fulfill his or her responsibilities in all the areas of life without neglecting any. This is not easy to do and takes time to learn. For young adults, it is easy to get overwhelmed because of a need for success in one area of life, causing them to let other areas slide. A woman raising children needs to have friends outside the home. A young man struggling to support his family needs to find time to be with them. Some people need to learn to work harder, while others need to learn to relax more. We need balance in our life since in the long run the balanced life is most rewarding.

Second, we must learn to concentrate on others more and self less. Because of our fallen state, it is natural to be egocentric and selfish. It is natural to get upset because of the frustration that life and people are causing. However, true happiness never comes from egocentrism and a view that everyone is picking on us. The only way to break out of this life of unhappiness is to begin to focus more on the needs of others. As we reach out to help others in need, we will find our own lives more enriched and satisfying.

13

Putting on the Whole Armor of God

One problem we have today in the church is an inadequate concept of Christian growth. We are very primitive in our ability to relate our Christian faith to practical issues of life experiences. This is why there is an attempt in the field of Christian psychology to integrate Biblical teachings with psychological concepts. It is not enough for us to label something as a sin if we are unable to describe the process by which it became a sin as well as tell a person specifically what he or she needs to do to overcome it. In other words, we must tell a person what specific sin has caused his or her psychological problem and not just say "there must be sin in your life." We also must be able to tell a person specifically how God can help him or her solve the problem and not just say "go pray about it." Because of an inadequately defined concept of man and the effects of sin on our personality, we have "copped out" by giving people pat answers that do nothing for them but lead to frustration. The Christian does as he or she was told and prays about it but, because of a lack of insight into the real problem, the problem does not go away. This leads either to doubt in self as to spirituality or doubt in God as to His ability to answer prayers. We failed in that we did not help the person become specific enough about the sin behind the problem. Our Christian theory of development will help us in this area.

Matthew 28:19 indicates that we are to "go and disciple all nations," however, in the church today we have changed the word "disciple"to the word "save." In other words, we have reduced our task to one of evangelism. The emphasis in the church is on getting people saved and our success is too often judged by how many converts go forward, rededications take place, or church memberships are transferred. The task is merely one of getting someone to go forward in a church service. While this is very important and the essential starting point of our faith, we cannot stop there or we end up with a church full of babes in Christ. To disciple means that we cannot stop at salvation and feel that our task is completed. The command of Christ is not fulfilled until we lead a person to the fullness of his or her maturity in Christ as it relates to his or her particular stage of development. Our Christian theory of development, then, provides us with a model of Christian growth so that we can help Christians become more than babes in Christ.

A few examples will illustrate our point. We discovered that there are two negative emotions which we all have stemming from the Nurturance Stage, and these are anxiety and frustration. We also found that the positive emotion associated with this stage is a feeling of peace or contentment. This leads us to see that when a Christian begins to worry about his or her future or what people think, this anxiety is a result of sin. The sin is one of an inability to believe that God will take care of our needs as He promised He would in the Bible. Anxiety is solved through acknowledgment of the unrealistic expectations we place on God and by giving up the will to egocentrism. In doing this, we will allow God to nurture us and the positive emotion of peace results. When we can look to God and not self or others as the source of supply for our needs, we find that He has promised to take care of us. Peace comes when we can accept God's nurturance, accept ourselves as we are, and allow God to work through other people to meet our needs.

A second example relates to the Obedience Stage. In this stage the negative emotional states are fear and anger and the positive emotion is faith. When, as Christian adults, we discover either fear or anger within us, we need to look to what we know about the Obedience Stage for our solution. As Christians, we know that perfect love casts out fear. This means that if we continue to have irrational fears, we are not allowing God to perfect us in love, and therefore we are not growing. Fear stems from the idea of doing something wrong and then being punished for it, which leads us to the sin of rebellion. Rebellion is the desire not to be punished and not to have to live within limits. The solution is to accept God's authority as legitimate and to be obedient and submissive to His commands. This also means that we must be submissive to those to whom God has delegated authority. The positive emotional state that results when we can accept the legitimacy of authority is the ability to trust or have faith.

A final example relates to the Behavior Stage. In this stage, the two negative emotions are shame and conceit. If we are to grow as Christians, the positive emotion that we are to replace these two with is that of humility. A person gets upset because he or she wants to be able to be irresponsible without being accountable. When you suggest to a person who has a problem with conceit that he or she is acting irresponsibly, he or she usually gets angry at you. The sin here is pride—the desire to be irresponsible without suffering any loss of happiness. This person grows when he or she is able to accept full responsibility for everything that he or she does. However, we must go one step further. As Christians, we are responsible but no longer accountable for our sin. In other words, we must accept God's imputed righteousness. The emotion of humility is experienced by the Christian when he or she discovers that salvation does not need to be earned. The hope of eternal life is not based on human works but on the work of Christ on the cross. As a result of this promise, we are able to discipline and train ourselves with less pressure to perform and always be the best.

The insight that we are establishing through these examples is that the stages of psychospiritual development that were presented are also the stages of spiritual growth and development. A babe in Christ must start at the Nurturance Stage and work his or her way through the order of stages regardless of age at Christian conversion. Any fixations that a person has had in the normal process of human growth and development will result in blocks to spiritual growth and development. In this way, we establish a well-developed process of Christian growth that derives its sequence from the broader concept of human growth. If, as we have suggested, no child is able to progress through childhood without some distortions in his or her development, the first step in the Unstage for a person who becomes a babe in Christ is to go back and resolve the distortions in development that arose during earlier childhood stages. The goal is to lead the person through these stages as it relates to a spiritual rather than a temporal solution. Parents can nurture, but only God can nurture so that all things work together for our good. The commands of parents can be culturally relative at times, but the commands of God are absolute and eternal. People can learn to be responsible to their society, but they must also learn that they have a greater responsibility to God. As human beings, we can attempt to discover love in marriage and friendships, but as Christians we discover that true love can only come from God. Each stage of human development, then, only can be completely resolved when it is faced in its spiritual dimension.

The main value in establishing a Christian theory of development is that it provides a framework through which we can become more effective in pointing out to people how God can meet their needs. Whether a person is a Christian or a non-Christian, he or she needs the Bible explained in terms of its ability to solve his or her existential struggles. If we are unable to do this, we turn Christianity into just another religion that makes a lot of promises but is never able to deliver. Through this theory, the Bible can become more relevant to us today and passages that used to seem abstract and vague now become clearer and more meaningful.

One important Scriptural passage that is able to become much less abstract as we relate it to our stages of development is found in Ephesians 6:13–17. This passage charges us to put on the whole armor of God and then gives the pieces of armor that we are to wear. Most people find this particular passage too vague. How are we to put on our spiritual armor if we do not know what the pieces represent? By relating each piece of armor to one of our spiritual stages of development, we can now become very specific as to how we can go about putting on the whole armor of God.

The verse that instructs us to have our feet shod with the *gospel of peace* relates to the Nurturance Stage. The positive emotion that is associated with the Nurturance Stage is peace. Peace results when we feel that we have security as an individual because someone cares about us and will take care of us. The armor covering our feet—the gospel of peace—is nothing more than to see God as the source of supply for our needs and believe that He will take care of us. If we really can believe that all things work together for good for a person who is a Christian and learn to praise and thank God for everything that happens to us, this gives us armor to withstand Satan's attacks in terms of anxiety and frustration. In this way, we have the gospel of peace through placing our *security in the providence of God.*

The verse related to the Obedience Stage is that which instructs us to take on the *shield of faith* by which we are able to quench all the fiery darts of the wicked. The shield of faith as armor is to be obedient to God as well as other authority figures ordained by God. The fiery darts in this verse relate to rebellion. Christians who find themselves being rebellious toward certain laws or commands of God have been hit with a fiery dart because they were unwilling to be obedient to God and, thereby, lacked the shield of faith. A Christian wife who resents or resists the command to be submissive to her husband has opened herself and her marriage to Satanic attack. The Christian father who does not train and discipline his children as God commands opens his family to spiritual warfare. The second step of spiritual growth is to develop an obedient heart which responds to the will of God. The shield of faith, then, is finding our *liberty under the sovereignty of God.*

The breastplate of righteousness relates to the Behavior Stage of development. Although a person cannot obtain eternal life through self-discipline and hard work, these attributes are important for our spiritual growth. The breastplate of righteousness is the ability to learn the Word of God and to discipline ourselves and work hard toward the fulfilling of the Great Commission. A person who does not have this breastplate is one who is shallow in his or her understanding of Biblical teachings and lazy in terms of the time that he or she is willing to give God in service. As Paul clearly tells us, we obtain our righteousness from God through grace, but James warns that we are in trouble if our faith does not eventually lead to works. The difference is that before a person is saved works relate to law, but after our salvation, works relate to love. We put on the breastplate of righteousness when we begin to develop *competency within the law of God* by following His commandments.

The fourth piece of armor is the *helmet of salvation,* and this is related to the Motive Stage. Our helmet of salvation is our belief in Jesus Christ as our Lord and Savior. When we are able to acknowledge Christ as Lord and Savior, we are able to restore ourselves to a right relationship with God. The important point in this process is not our acceptance of Christ, but God's acceptance of us. Through the helmet of salvation, we are able to use the name of Jesus to obtain spiritual power in our lives. Through the helmet of salvation, we can gain victory over Satanic attacks upon us. If we truly believe in Jesus as our Lord, we can draw upon the power of His Lordship when we ask and do things in His Name. The helmet of salvation, then, is the power that we obtain as we receive *acceptance through the grace of God.*

The fifth piece of armor is to have our *loins girt about with truth,* and this relates to the Meaning Stage. Jesus Christ came to give us the truth so that the truth could set us free. Ignorance and lies enslave people, but when people can face the world and themselves as they really are without needing to hide, they truly become free. The truth is that man without God is not immortal but will someday die. The truth is that Man did not evolve and progress through human effort, but was created by God who controls all that happens in the world. The belt of truth is that there is a difference in life between serving ourselves and serving God. The only way that life can have real meaning is by living the truth, which only comes through a commitment of our life to the cause of Christ. If we really believe we have the truth, we need to share it with others. As a result, having our loins girt with truth comes through our *commitment to sharing the Word of God*—Jesus Christ—with the people around us.

The sixth stage is the Intimacy Stage and the piece of armor related to this stage is the *sword of the Spirit,* which is love. Jesus summed up the whole Bible in the commandments that we are to love God with all of our heart, soul, and mind that we are to love our neighbor as we love ourselves. The sword of the Spirit that is given to us by the Holy Spirit when we become Christians is the capacity to love; the ability to love self, neighbor, and God. As we grow to the point where we truly can begin to love, we pick up our sword of the Spirit. The Bible tells us that the Word of God is sharper than any physical sword and its power comes through love. The love of God, when experienced by a person, completely disarms him or her. As we share the Gospel message with others, the best weapon we can have is the love that we have for people. The only thing that destroys our ability to love is sin, which means that as we have unconfessed sin in our life we lose the sword of the Spirit. In this stage, a mature Christian is one who can be attacked and still respond in love. Our sword of the Spirit, therefore, involves having *intimacy in the presence of God.*

The final stage of development is the Fruit Stage and the final piece of armor is that which we use as we *stand before the throne of God*— "That you may be able to stand in the evil day and having done all to stand (v. 13)." As discussed earlier, every person someday must stand before God and give an accounting for his or her life. The question before us concerns how our life is to be evaluated. This book presents the idea that the only thing that we will have to defend us at God's judgment is the good fruit that we have produced with our lives. If our lives have produced no fruit or evil fruit, we will stand unarmed, naked before God. Fruit, then is our final weapon, and it is through good fruit that we will have *value at the judgment of God.*

The final challenge of this book is that we work together as Christians to discover the truth of God. The world does not need solutions to problems that are not ultimately satisfying. The world does not need a psychology that only helps sick people adjust to a sick social order. The world needs a Christian psychology that helps people resolve their psychological conflicts in relation to their sin and then leads them on to positive growth. The world needs a Christian psychology that will help each person become the fullness of his or her potential as created in the image of God. Through the Christian developmental theory presented in this book, I have attempted to present the truth—a truth that is real; a truth that can change lives. I recognize that there is much work that still needs to be done. These ideas need to be debated. These ideas need to be researched. In the process of study, research, and debate, some of the ideas presented here may need to be changed or even discarded. However, if through this process we are able to better know the truth of God and use it to help people, the effort will have been worthwhile.

PUT ON THE WHOLE ARMOR OF GOD (Ephesians 6:13–17)

1. Nurturance — "Feet shod with the preparation of the Gospel of peace."
   Security in the **Providence** of God.

2. Obedience — "Taking the shield of faith wherewith you shall be able to quench all the fiery darts of the wicked."
   Liberty under the **Sovereignty** of God.

3. Behavior — "Having on the breastplate of righteousness."
   Competency within the **Law** of God.

4. Motive — "Take the helmet of salvation."
   Acceptance through the **Grace** of God.

5. Meaning — "Stand, having your loins girt about with truth."
   Commitment to the **Word** of God.

6. Love — "Take the sword of the Spirit."
   Intimacy in the **Presence** of God.

7. Fruit — "That you may be able to withstand in the evil day and having done all to stand."
   Value at the **Judgement** of God.

Index

215

217

Psychospiritual stages of human
development (*see* Behavior Stage;
Fruit Stage; Innocence Stage; Love
Stage; Meaning Stage; Motive
Stage; Nurturance Stage;
Obedience Stage)
Punishment, 72, 81, 124

Radicals, 147–48
Rage, 72
Rebellion, 73, 97, 115–16, 124, 209,
211
Rebellious child state, 116, 117, 120,
148–49
Red Sea, crossing, 122
Regression, 179
Rejection, fear of, 112, 124
Repentance, 95
Responsibility, 116–18, 178
in Behavior Stage, 78–87
in Fruit Stage, 178–81
in Innocence Stage, 38–40
in Love Stage, 158–62
in Meaning Stage, 142–47
in Motive Stage, 98–106
in Nurturance Stage, 45–52
in Obedience Stage, 60–67
Revelation, 60
Role Call of God, 195, 198–201
Romance, 155
Romans, 6, 8, 77, 78, 97, 131
Ruth, 44

I Samuel, 98, 195
Satan, 119, 120, 122
School system, 67, 76, 77, 79–81
Searching child state, 121, 149
Security, need for, 14, 18, 52
Self, search for, 122–24
Self-actualization, 12–13, 96, 119
Self-esteem:
in Behavior Stage, 86, 90, 91
in Fruit Stage, 185–86
in Love Stage, 166–68
in Meaning Stage, 149
in Motive Stage, 109–10
in Nurturance Stage, 53
in Obedience Stage, 63, 64, 70

Selfishness, 158
Separation, 124
Shame, 92, 124, 209
Sheltered dependency, 53, 69
Sin, 54–57, 73, 93, 112, 121–24,
150, 152–53, 171–72, 207–9,
213
Skepticism, 171
Social conscience, 158, 162
Social involvement, 183, 184
Social roles, 136–38, 150
Spanking, 60, 63, 72, 85
Special Call of God, 195, 201–2
Spiritual origin, 32–34
Suicide, 169–70
Superiority, 91, 92, 124
Supervisory dependency, 69

Tantrums, 73
Teenagers, 8, 18, 96–113, 123, 124
Ten Commandments, 7
I Thessalonians, 44, 193
I Timothy, 176
II Timothy, 78
Transcendence, 185

Unconditional nurturance, 50–51
Unity, 184–85
Unstage, 114–33, 196, 197
crossing the Jordan, 128–29
crossing the Red Sea, 121–22
Exodus analogy, 118–20
wilderness experience, 122–28

Value in life, 18, 182–85
Values, 83–84, 86
internalization of, 126–27
transmission, 179
Violence, 111
Vision, 144, 145–46

Weakness, 71–72, 124
Wilderness experience, 122–28
Wisdom, 180–81, 200
Women's liberation movement, 138,
152
Women's rights, 41
Work satisfaction, 182, 184